GOD's PLAN

Finding His
Best For
Your Life

MIKE FRANSEN

Copyright © 2024 by Mike Fransen
First Paperback Edition

All rights reserved. No part of this publication may be reproduced, distributed, or transmitted in any form or by any means, including photocopying, recording, or other electronic or mechanical methods, without the prior written permission of the publisher, except in the case of brief quotations embodied in critical reviews and certain other noncommercial uses permitted by copyright law. For permission requests, write to the publisher, addressed "Attention: Permissions Coordinator," at the address below.

Some names, businesses, places, events, locales, incidents, and identifying details inside this book have been changed to protect the privacy of individuals.

Published by Freiling Agency, LLC.

P.O. Box 1264
Warrenton, VA 20188

www.FreilingAgency.com

PB ISBN: 978-1-963701-21-0
E-book ISBN: 978-1-963701-22-7

TO THE COUNTLESS PEOPLE I discovered after writing *The Legacy Business*, who were so encouraging and inspiring as they crave and seek God-inspired lives and are digging in to understand how that looks for them. They helped me to realize and appreciate that "all-in" means just that. I needed to write this book because I needed this kick in the pants as my knees started to get a little wobbly as I encountered temporary earthly stress and discomfort in the pursuit of my life fully under the control of God. Once again, my best friend and wife, Stacey, fully embraced and supported this effort in a busy season of life. Like almost everything over the last twenty-plus years, I could not do it without her. Seeing our daughters transitioning from girls to godly, all-in on fire women is a tremendous source of strength of inspiration for this project. I am humbled and grateful to be called their dad.

CONTENTS

Preface	Punctuation That Count	vii
1	Godly Education	1
2	Ironman Approach	7
3	Needed – My Mustard Seed	11
4	May I Take Your Order Please?	15
5	Hedging Gone Wrong	19
6	My Plan – The Ultimate Ponzi Scheme	23
7	Life Insurance Killer – Life Giver	27
8	God's Chop Shop	31
9	Smoothie King	35
10	Business Plan Rewrite	41
11	Asymmetric	47
12	Holy Tap-out	51
13	No Cheating	55
14	God Cares So Much	59
15	Don't Bench God	63
16	Lead-out Rider	69
17	Bragging Rights	73
18	Joint Operation	79
19	Reach and Pull	85
20	Travel Light	91
21	Loving the Joneses Instead of Keeping Up with Them	97
22	Looking Back to Look Ahead	101
23	Catch and Release	107
24	Take Your Time and Hurry Up	111

25	Kingly Lessons	115
26	Super Model	121
27	One Degree Off	125
28	The Answer Is Yes	129
29	Expect a Fight – Stay in the Fight	133
30	Turn-by-Turn Navigation	139
31	Contentment in the Journey	143
32	Piles on the Side of the Road	147
33	Family Planning	151
34	Clicks and Sticks	157

PREFACE

PUNCTUATION THAT COUNTS

"For I know the plans I have for you," declares the Lord, "plans to prosper you and not to harm you, plans to give you hope and a future."

Jeremiah 29:11

CAN ONE PUNCTUATION MARK at the end of a certain three-word clause really make a profound difference in my life and yours? I think it has and will. Those two marks are the question mark and exclamation mark, placed on the end of the phrase "This is it." Attack this life—my life—with all the gusto I can muster and a plan that is 100 percent mine (really anything more than 0 percent), and there is a wildly unsatisfying "?" waiting for me at the end. However, if I can give up control of the steering wheel of "my" life and "my" map, I go well beyond my limited capabilities to the place where only God can lead with the simple but profoundly satisfying "!".

We live in a world that in its careful quest to remove God from the equation and elevate the created above the Creator, has unsurprisingly found its way into chaos, pandemic levels of selfishness, and endless emptiness. Entire companies and marketing efforts are built around the notion of us not letting anyone get in the way of our lives, our decisions, and our desires. This experiment has been well documented throughout history and in my opinion has experienced a 0 percent success rate. I don't know about you, but I want that exclamation point at the end of "this is it" now more than ever. Even as a Christian, my human tendencies and controlling nature are at odds with allowing "my" life to be steered by someone else.

It is tension and juxtaposition I must embrace and actually seek to live in. This should not come as a surprise given the same God instructs us to do seemingly outlandish things like loving our enemies. The arrow that shoots the straightest and furthest comes from the string on the bow and has the most tension in it. I want to be launched into this life as far as my Creator intended, so I need to be ok thriving and struggling in the tension that makes this possible. I believe I am in good company in this quest, and as I pen many of these ideas around plans and purpose, my prayer is that you come along with me on this journey to become passionate and reinvigorated in the pursuit of all that God intended for each of our lives.

1

GODLY EDUCATION

NEAR THE END OF 2017, God began the gut-wrenching process of equipping me with what author and pastor Steve Farrar referred (*Finishing Strong*) to as a master's degree in Character Acquisition (MCA). While I had been praying for and feeling a tugging to change some things, I fell into this education somewhat involuntarily. It began in a subtle but unusual fashion. I had finally received one of those supposedly coveted job titles that has "chief" in it. We were finishing up some ambitious but successful projects and I was feeling accomplished (which in and of itself should have alarmed me). But I very distinctly felt God saying that for 2018 I needed to focus on "staying humble and kind." That seemed odd since I aspired to always be respectful and kind to everyone and in almost comical fashion was quietly proud of how humble I was. What I did not know at that moment about 2018 was that the wheels for me professionally were going to start coming off. As the year went on, my normal hard work and diligence could not overcome things beyond my control. By the end of that long year, I was exhausted, and it became easy to get short with people and feel pride gurgling up inside of me. This process kick-started a multi-year journey working toward my "MCA" degree. With each passing year and obstacle, God has gradually matured me by prying my fingers off the steering wheel to allow my life to more fully conform to His intended purpose. To say this process has been hard would be a gross understatement.

Toward the end of 2018 around the same time as the previous year, again, I felt very distinctly that God's words for me for 2019 were "new beginnings." This was particularly unnerving because the implication was that there was going to be an ending. In my very logical, hopeful mind, I assumed God would cleanly wrap up my current job and right on my ideal timeline, bring into plain sight a superior option with all the magical corporate and financial trimmings. Once again, my need for further spiritual education proved great. What I can now appreciate is this "new beginning" means something vastly different in God's planning. 2019 would indeed represent the end of my time with a firm that I had worked at for thirteen years. However, the beginning was not some new job but rather a new reset (and beginning) with my family, how I thought about work, and more broadly how I approached life.

By the end of 2019, despite being the slow learner I can be, I caught on to God's increasingly less subtle approach and was anticipating what word would come next. The phrase that came to me for 2020 was simply "stay faithful". Even now, knowing what we all now know about 2020, it is really amazing to think about His providence. While the immediate, clean, new job opportunity had proved elusive in 2019, my initial thought was that I just needed to lean into God a little harder for 2020 and let Him guide. By March and April, with Covid throwing me (and all of us) into a confused tailspin, I knew this two-word phrase would prove to be absolutely essential to my mental, emotional, and spiritual health.

Late in 2020, with my next professional chapter still feeling anything but clear, I started to notice something. When I let Him, God was able to use my increasing reliance on Him despite that uncertainty to connect with others. Many people I encountered during this time seemed unsettled. As much as the "my-life-my-plan" version of me would have loved to isolate until I had a really clean success story to share, people connected much better with the incomplete version of me that was open about my ongoing growth. The word going into 2021 was "peace and joy." These two qualities proved more elusive for me in this season than I wanted to admit. As a friend said one time, "Men tend to have two primary emotions they have to combat: fear and anger." In seeking very specifically peace and joy, God gifted me with the exact two things I needed in order to offset these two tendencies in times of uncertainty and loss of control.

The word "reveal" was God's word for me in 2022. In typical God fashion, it was way more vague than I would like. But now, with the benefit of two more years into my "MCA" degree, I had come to appreciate more and more about how God works. He knows me well—He knows all of us well—which makes sense because He hand built each of us uniquely and purposely. My life remains absolutely my life, and free will is still completely at my disposal. However, I am now more comfortable operating from the place where I am following His plan exclusively for my life—His will but my choice.

In the same way that God's intended purpose for *The Legacy Business* was to remind and encourage me and others to embrace and thrive in the privilege of leaning into God to live beyond ourselves, the nudging I have for this simple four-word-titled book and theme is to serve as a reminder of the tension we must all eventually choose to live in if we are to reach all that God intends for us. In my human nature, I so badly want to hold onto the illusion of control of "my plan" for "my life." But the master creator of everything turns out to know best. Even more encouraging is the idea that He in fact wants this for me more than I could even want it for myself. He's just waiting for me (and you) to ask. With this book and MCA process, I trust I am finally fully embracing the entire plan God has for my life. I pray and trust anyone reading these words can also come to the same conclusion because, frankly, the world, more than ever, desperately needs Christians to be in full alignment with this heaven-oriented plan.

2

IRONMAN APPROACH

SOMEWHERE ALONG THE LINE, our daughters decided that we would make our way through most of the Marvel Movie series. Among the action-packed movies in this series is the Ironman storyline. The mad-scientist and hero feverishly works to perfect the failproof suit that enables him to fearlessly waltz around and save the world. Absent this suit, he is very pedestrian and frankly, as a movie watcher, not very compelling. But once the suit comes on and danger is running rampant, suddenly Ironman becomes a must-watch.

It turns out that there is an Ironman in the Bible, too. His name is Samson. If you know the story of his life, you know he possessed superhuman strength unlike almost anyone else mentioned in the Bible (and history). Instead of a suit, it was his uncut hair that God allowed to be the source of his unusual strength. But Samson had a problem that is unfortunately familiar to many of us that share his human tendencies. Even though he had a God-given gift, Samson was determined to follow the "my-life-my-plan" roadmap. As a result, his story was packed full of non-stop bad choices in and around the short-lived superhero feats as he spiraled downward. Samson was determined to live his life exactly according to his plan. Ultimately, despite one of the most compelling and enviable Ironman-like suits in history, his nearly complete failure to leverage his life following God's plan rendered him an almost forgotten character. In fact, I'm not convinced Samson's name would even crack most people's top twenty or thirty from the Bible.

It is interesting and fun to imagine a little about what could have been with Samson in total alignment with God's plan for his life. Just imagine—if little old David could take down Goliath with a slingshot, how epic would the stories about Samson have been? There might have been an entire, historically accurate Marvel Movie series just around all of his God-sponsored conquests. But there aren't—just one last tragic footnote that abruptly ends his squandered existence on Earth.

It is always so much easier for me to spot these things in other people. However, I find God to be the master mirror builder. In the Bible, God has so flawlessly articulated examples like that of Samson which, without fail, reveal something glaring in my own life. When it comes to how to process my approach to life, I am more like Samson than I want to admit. God has placed me (and all of us) in situations with given talents. Like Samson, it is easy to use these gifts as a way to advance my own agenda without ever pausing and simply asking God, the source of all things, why He gave them to me and how He intends for them to be used. "I've got this" seems like a reasonable and even honorable statement in today's culture, but when I view them through the example of Samson, I realize what I'm calling self-reliance is more often than not really just flawed and selfish actions birthed out of pride.

I don't know about you, but I want to live the richest and fullest life that God planned for me. I want the suit always "on" and those God-sponsored dreadlocks untouched. I want to tap into every ounce of power He's committed to sending for my life's direction. In this fallen and broken world, I have come to terms with not being anywhere close to an easy or cruise control life. Rather, I desire a fully engaged existence with the Lord that is leveraging my humanity while on Earth to focus only on things of eternal value. What about you?

3

NEEDED – MY MUSTARD SEED

And He said to them, "Because of the littleness of your faith; for truly I say to you, if you have faith the size of a mustard seed, you will say to this mountain, 'Move from here to there,' and it will move; and nothing will be impossible to you.
Matthew 17:20

JESUS IS THE ULTIMATE word picture artist, and He has the gift of gracefully, yet bluntly, helping us visualize our limited abilities compared to His limitless and masterful talents and plans for us. When it comes to framing the power of our lives under the direction of His plan, the mustard seed analogy is among the most telling, convicting, yet hopefully encouraging story. I can almost see Jesus calmly picking up a nearly invisible mustard seed as He detects the lack of faith (i.e., confidence) in those gathered around Him. They all likely had to lean in to even detect what Jesus just put into His hand, yet He calmly but confidently says, "See that? Not much at all, right? You have no idea what I could do with 'all-in' faith that was this size. See that mountain over there? Faith even this small could move a mountain that big." Every word in the Bible, but especially those in red, where we see direct quotes from Jesus, is intentional, and these are no different.

First, Jesus acknowledged how naturally small and weak the faith muscle is in humans. If we cannot touch it and see it, we struggle to make sense of it, let alone believe in it. The gap between my faith retention and its application is surprisingly greater than I would like many times. By this I mean I can walk into church on Sunday, be completely mesmerized and blown away by someone who shares an amazing, personal faith story in the moment I feel inspired and ready for action. However, in just a few short moments, my disposition and rock-solid faith can waver. I can be walking out of church and one text that is personal to my world throws me for a loop. I find myself quickly reverting back to "oh no, this bad—what will I do? This could go poorly." Just like that, I have affirmed that my faith in the Creator of all things can make a nearly invisible seed in Jesus's hand look like a boulder.

Second, I love the throw-down imagery Jesus uses in Matthew. It is almost like He is playing the most important and life-giving of all truth or dare games.

Needed – My Mustard Seed

He is begging us to test Him—to simply give him ALL the faith we have so that He can show off. For most of us showing off is just that: leveraging a moment to make sure all the lights are shining back on ourselves. However, in the ultimate God move, He is asking us to trust Him to do huge things, via His plan for us so our lives are forever changed and all of the goodness points others back to the Source, Jesus. It really is brilliant. We get to take no credit, which allows us to stay on mission, at peace and with joy, and all the while watching in amazement the mountains He is moving in and through our lives.

Finally, I see once again in Jesus someone who is wildly for me and is begging me to ask for His help to tap into His endless power. This becomes my big challenge and obstacle—to not let pride, fear, or whatever else limits my faith prevent me from simply and sincerely asking. To carry this metaphor further, I am afraid that sometimes not only am I not moving mountains or even asking God for anything close to that. I am in fact standing at the base of the mountain, frustratingly kicking rocks on the ground wondering what's wrong with me and at a loss. I love the simplicity of what James says in James 4:2-3, "You do not have because you do not ask God. When you ask, you do not receive, because you ask with the wrong motives, that you may spend what you get on your pleasures."

I need to be reminded on a daily basis that if I want to be in alignment with the "move-mountains" kind-of-plan, the kind that results in fulfillment, then I need to take God up on this offer to lean into Him with the right heart and let Him do His best work through and in me.

What I love in general about the stories about Jesus and the disciples is that all of us can relate to the disciples and their humanity. They were trying to make sense of so many things, learn from the long-announced Messiah who was nothing like they expected, and ultimately be responsible for the massive worldwide movement known as Christianity. These men became absolute mountain movers. This story is told immediately after they had been defeated and unable to cast a demon out. But Jesus, always ready to coach them up, leverages this seemingly small moment, fully knowing the absolute warriors this group would become, to plant in each of them a small seed that would take root and ultimately blossom. I need to be reminded that the small and often discouraging lessons God is coaching me through may in fact be the necessary ingredients required for the future big plans He has for me—if I am so inclined. I pray that I am and always will be. Will you?

4

MAY I TAKE YOUR ORDER PLEASE?

TACTICAL MISSIONS IN THE military, when executed at their highest level, save lives and accomplish critical tasks. Even as a mundane-sounding finance officer in the Army, the basic process for missions worked no different. I would receive an order from above, ask relevant and clarifying questions, and prepare and request the necessary resources needed. I would then go out and execute the plan, with frequent updates communicated back to the source of the orders. It was often the case that my mission was part of a much larger coordinated effort, with my success or failure affecting other missions. At the end of every mission, it is not only customary but critical to sit down and do what the military calls an "After Action Review". It is from this place of transparency that growth and future improvements result. But there are a couple of ingredients needed for successful missions that I find are critical, to an even deeper level, in my life and to be in full compliance with God's will for it.

First, I have to acknowledge who outranks whom. It is anti-twenty-first century to think of us submitting to the will and desires of someone besides ourselves; but, one of the big concessions I had to make by becoming a Christian was the explicit acknowledgement that there is a God, and it is not me. This loving God, who created everything I will ever see has full visibility on the past, present, and future and is best qualified to direct the mission for my life. If the military realizes that its best chance for success relies on an explicit chain of command, even one that has imperfect people capable of occasional misguided directives, it seems very reasonable, if not obvious, that I should be very comfortable following the lead of the Creator of the universe Who's still mistake free.

Second, constant communication is key. Missions are too important to leave to chance, and the one thing I never saw during my time in the military was a casual approach to missions with infrequent check-ins. In fact, the opposite was true. The better communication and resulting missions go in the military, the more confident leadership has to give missions of increased complexity and importance to certain people and teams. It is not an accident that we, as a country, trust the absolute most critical missions to the most elite teams who communicate and execute the best. It is somewhat surprising that having lived this on so many levels in life, this remains such an area of constant growth opportunity for me. I have often heard that communication in the Christian life often looks like God speaking to us through the Bible with us communicating to Him via prayer; but, at a much deeper level and arguably with higher stakes than military missions, the absence of this two-way communication can't help but leave my life in a lurch, constantly struggling to stay on God's course and avoiding the countless distractions and pitfalls the world will gladly offer up daily.

Finally, and encouragingly, as Christians, we have been gifted with the one thing the military could never hope to offer, even in the most favorable circumstances: a complete and guaranteed victory. We know our eternity is secured, leaving our impact for God and His glory the only unresolved issue. I, unfortunately, often live acting and behaving defeated. But as challenging as it is to allow human nature and worldly distractions to get in the way of being on mission, in reality, with the weight of ultimate outcome already solved for, it should be incredibly freeing. God wants me to enjoy this place of freedom, not out of any misperception that victory has anything to do with anything I have or will do, but out of a place of overwhelming gratitude that wants to draw as many others as possible into this same victory. When I rest in this, the deafening noise and chaos of the world around me dissipates and I am able to focus more clearly on the mission God has designed for me inside of His bigger plan.

Missions are great. They provide us with purpose and action, but they also require the humility and maturity that recognizes they are bigger than us. It requires accountability, and by nature, is challenging and exhausting. In this sharpening and pruning process, God continues to use in my life, He simply asks me each day to lay down my thoughts and ideas for where *I* want to go and replace it with a far better one that He pre-planned for me. He will allow me to make this choice and graciously work with me to pick up the pieces when I stubbornly plow ahead. But why fight the Author and Creator of the universe and all missions when I can simply and prayerfully come alongside Him and actively seek His mission on the way to ultimate and complete victory at the end of my life?

5

HEDGING GONE WRONG

"So, because you are lukewarm—neither hot nor cold—I am about to spit you out of my mouth."
Revelation 3:16

THERE ARE MANY TIMES in life where it is prudent, if not responsible, to have a couple of varied courses of action thought out. In other words, you hedge between alternatives in order to not become overexposed to any particular one. However, when it comes to God's economy and how He feels about our approach to living our one life on Earth, this verse in Revelation leaves no room for interpretation. He desperately wants 100 percent of us to conform to His will for our lives. While His desire for us is unequivocally for us to follow Him completely, in this verse He seems to hammer home a point by inferring that He'd prefer us to be 100 percent in on our own plans than being lukewarm and hedging by living a mix of the two. That is less destructive to His overall mission of reaching all people. I am learning, true to form of our logical and practical God, that there are a couple of highly relevant reasons for singular focus in my life.

First, I'm a terrible multi-tasker, as it seems we actually all are. Luke 16:13 reminds of this when it simply states, "You can't serve two masters." In the context of this book, it unfortunately means that a life lived constantly straddling the fence between "my plan for my life" versus "God's plan for my life" becomes impossible to manage. However, I have discovered the reason God can't stomach this duplicity is that on the other side of the equation, "my" plan is actually Satan's plan. This sounds harsh, and while I would like to think a little bit better about myself and my master-planning capabilities, the truth is my plan involves self-service, materialism, instant gratification, and other common tools in the devil's toolbox. The one thing that draws us eventually into a relationship with God is His holiness, which will never ever be compatible with any of the enemy's qualities. The moment God compromises on any of these would be the exact moment He would no longer be worth following.

Second, I have learned that operating in lukewarm waters causes mass casualties. When we read stories of some of the recent wars, one of the more challenging scenarios soldiers had to contend with was not being able to identify friend from foe. The tribal member you had coffee with and discussed building a new school with at lunch was part of the same group that ambushed you the next day. I recently watched a movie that depicted this scenario, and it was hard to watch as trust deteriorated, suspicion escalated and with each subsequent interaction the risk to everyone was elevated. Rarely do I view my own lukewarm tendencies through this destructive lens, but it in fact is a pretty accurate analogy. The longer I mislead myself into thinking I am successfully picking and choosing my spots in life where it's "me and my plans" versus God's plan, the greater risk I am putting myself and others at.

Finally, in my hedging and lukewarm efforts, I become totally ineffective in fulfilling my part in God's larger mission for all Christians. In its purest form, as a Christian, I should conform to His plan and point others to Christ through my words and actions. I certainly never want the title of hypocrite assigned to me. But isn't hedging or being lukewarm the epitome of the definition of having severe misalignment between words and actions? In doing that, we run the risk of not only confusing the very audience of the world we are called to reach, but perhaps more devastatingly, building walls and creating resentment that becomes even harder for those who might come behind us to overcome. Thankfully, the same God that used a marching band to cause the walls of Jericho to fall is more than capable. I just know that for me, I want to be part of that solution and not a hindrance.

Freedom and power, as words and terms, just sound invigorating. These are tools I want defining me and my life. Tell me how to get these in large quantities, and I'm going to be listening. I've got my pen and several empty pages ready for notes. It turns out God only needed a couple of lines in Luke and Revelation: Go all in and long on Me and me alone— no compromises, no gaps, no hedges. We live in a "prove it" world, and as the saying goes, proof is in the pudding of our own lives. As Christians, in a fallen world and with imperfect human tendencies, we can all find plenty of proof of how quickly this goes off the rails. Thankfully, there is also overwhelming proof of "all-in" and "hot" lives where power, freedom, peace, and joy are the outputs of a life lived out under God's plan for it.

6

MY PLAN – THE ULTIMATE PONZI SCHEME

WE CAN ALL REMEMBER hearing some of the more epic and historic Ponzi Schemes like that of the famous and infamous Bernie Madoff. These are the empty promises of guaranteed, too-good-to-be-true, riskless returns on your investment. Through the lens of hindsight and a two-hour made-for-television recap, it is easy to cast judgment on anyone foolish enough to fall for something so blatantly deceptive and obviously doomed. However, usually there is a secondary reaction that can induce you to want to question everything you're invested in or involved with. Am I a victim to something like this right now? But if you think Bernie was slick, that is nothing compared to the next-level deceptiveness that Satan, the grand master of deceit, embarks on when he convinces us that our own life plan, not God's, is the winning one. Eve may have been the first to fall for one of these schemes in the Garden of Eden, but she was not the last. My ability to know this risk of insisting on "my" plan and preemptively put God's full plan into action will curb the extensive damage of falling victim to the "My Plan Ponzi Scheme."

Bernie and others who have crafted and executed these Ponzi schemes actually need what you have worse than you could ever need what they are promising. Without a steady stream of resources continuing to flow in from unsuspecting victims, the scheme ends relatively quickly. Sure, a few people get a little back in return early on but only as a means to extract more money from even more people. How many people have we read and heard about who tragically and eventually gave over their entire net worth, only to discover they might as well have lit it all on fire? I fear this is sometimes where I am susceptible to go directionally, when I blindly buy into the devil's scheme for the roadmap for my life. If we can just get into this school, get this job, follow this career path, marry this person, or buy this car, then "this" would bring about meaning or fulfillment. However, my continued investment of limited time and efforts in these pursuits, absent any directional guidance from God, guarantees a life depleted of purpose and peace.

My Plan – The Ultimate Ponzi Scheme

I remember when I was in business school and Stacey and I were still relatively new to the married game, we were resource light and had to be creative in how we did things, like going away for the weekend. When we were enticed for a free two-night stay in one of our favorite northeast coast towns in exchange for enduring—I mean sitting through—a timeshare sales pitch, we excitedly jumped at the opportunity. Using our best newlywed communication efforts, we both agreed ahead of time that no matter how compelling the pitch, we would resist its magnetic pull no matter what. I think I may have even had us practice saying "no thank you" out loud. Sure enough, about fifteen minutes in after a very compelling diagnosis of our desired and projected traveling habits for the next fifty years, the chatty salesman strategically left us alone for a minute. That turned out to be just enough time for Stacey to immediately turn to me and ask excitedly, "What do you think?" I reminded her of our plan, and we managed to have a great weekend and escape with our tiny wallet intact. To be clear, if this had been a car dealer, I would have been asking Stacey that question—we all have vulnerabilities. And no, I don't think timeshares are a Ponzi Scheme. But what I did learn out of this experience is that even though I may have committed to following God's plan and resisting the things about this world that try to convince me that my

God's Plan

plan will work, this does not mean that we won't be frequently confronted with new and "sweet-sounding" twists on the same "my-life-my-plan" scheme.

The dirty little secret that seems to perpetuate every Ponzi is the sprinkling of truth buried inside of the larger lie. That's what pulls us in and keeps us hooked as long as we are. Fortunately, as Christians, we are blessed because unlike being discerning on our financial investments when choosing which plan for our lives we will commit to, God's plan has a 100 percent success rate with countless five-star reviews and testimonials. It sounds almost irreverent to put it into this context, but for me, just seeing it framed this way reminds me just how irrational it is for me not to move forward under His failproof plan available to all of us. To be clear, what I continue to appreciate more and more is that this perfect plan does not equate too easy, conventional, or monetary. But what it does do when I'm in perfect alignment with Him is match my God-given talents and desires with His perfect plan for all of these.

7

LIFE INSURANCE KILLER – LIFE GIVER

ABOUT A YEAR OR so after having our second daughter, Sophie, our negative net worth suddenly meant something different. As much as I did not want to contemplate our daughters suddenly being parentless, it became clear that we owed it to them to at least take the just-in-case steps to ensure that there would be the necessary resources available for them to get started in life. We secured life insurance for Stacey and me. Not surprisingly, insurance companies arguably hope you live a long time, even more than you do for yourself. Predictably, they ask you a series of probing lifestyle questions to make sure you're not living in such a way that you're inviting a premature end to your life. As someone not crazy about heights, I was actually somewhat relieved to learn that sky diving, bungy jumping, and base jumping were heavily frowned upon if you want affordable rates. The reason they dread these activities so much is that there are just a couple pieces of equipment standing between you and an activated life insurance policy. The statistical reality is that there is a significant enough failure rate of the equipment (or general risks of these activities) resulting in an inevitable life ending impact waiting on the other end which is just enough to make the adjusters nervous.

If I am really honest—the kind of honest I measure by thoughts and not just words—I sometimes approach God's plan like the equipment needed for skydiving and bunging jumping. I develop a paralyzing fear of 100 percent commitment of jumping into alignment with His plan because I actually think His plan could fail me and have me splatting on the ground, with life in complete shambles. In fact, there are always going to be life insurance-like people in my life who fuel this thought and make me prone to second guessing the conviction around my faith walk.

The reality is that operating under my own extremely miniscule set of capabilities is really like jumping out of a plane without equipment on at all. The ride might be thrilling for a second, but the end result is no less problematic. Under God's plan, He becomes infinitely more than just a parachute and a safe landing. He possesses a bottomless well of any and all resources needed to not just freefall safely but thrive and flourish in any and every circumstance. In a world where we are presented with two, and only two, distinct choices about navigating life, I can't help but be a little sheepish when thinking about how easily I tend to opt for this freefall option.

So why do I do it? My observation in today's confused and troubled world is that when we look around, most people, even Christians, are in the "my plan free fall." This is why trying to measure our spiritual progress by using a human measuring stick is hopeless. It really does not matter if I am freefalling slightly slower than the person next to me – we're all headed to the same end state. I have realized with age and hopefully spiritual maturing, that I want to be the person that is shooting by the freefalling masses under full control of the God-driven jet pack. I get to take zero credit for the God-ordained life-giving plan but the beauty found is an endless supply where that came from. God's fulfillment center has never failed to deliver on any sincere request anyone has ever made to follow His plan.

8

GOD'S CHOP SHOP

OF ALL THE FORGETTABLE things reality television has offered us over the years, some of the more intriguing shows have centered around customized vehicles. These shows provide most of us a window into a world we otherwise would never see. The big personalities and uniquely talented teams take one-of-a-kind orders and transform ordinary looking vehicles into valuable pieces of art. It is always so fun to watch the amazed and enthusiastic reactions at the reveal. There is a reason there are no shows that show a typical assembly line of the same vehicle being made repeatedly. It might in fact be necessary to mass produce cars that satisfy basic driving needs, but we all seem to inherently crave things that are distinctly *us*.

Here is the funny thing I have noticed about "my plan." This same person—me—who is so intrigued by customization and one-of-a-kind things somehow ends up pursuing a plan for my life if I am not careful that merely morphs into a cheap imitation of someone else's life I have seen from a distance. I see the shiny objects, the perceived success and accolades, and do my best to replicate them for myself. For sure, there are many aspects of life that benefit from refined processes and methodologies that are smart to follow.

When it comes to creating a roadmap for our lives, there is no one more creative, capable and keenly interested in the process and end product of our lives than God. He created each of us with a custom set of cultural settings, skills and aptitude, and passions and interests. The only thing I believe He enjoys more than putting a set of raw materials here on Earth is getting the green light from each of us once we accept Him into our lives. We get to work using all of the parts He put together to live a life in full conformity with His intended purpose. Can you imagine getting to the end of one of these reality shows, and during the big reveal, the cloth on the car is removed; as everyone looks, it is clear that the car is unique—but in all the wrong ways. It is a mess and incomplete doesn't even begin to describe the vehicle. When the "what-happened-here" questions are asked, all the experts can say is the truth: "The owner of this vehicle thought they knew better than us and tried to help us. It is their car, so we let them go with it."

What makes the personalities in these chop shops so enduring is the almost emotional connection they make with the vehicles that they work on. It is personal, and they work feverishly and diligently to get each and every part of the project just right. There are unique obstacles and problems that put the whole project at risk, but they push forward and solve for them. If someone with long hair and tattoos can care that much about a car, how is it, as a Christian, that I have such a hard time accepting God's infinitely greater level of care and skill-crafting in executing the plan for my life? I suspect for me, it is my human frailty and need to be accepted by other humans who are following their own plans. I would many times rather compromise that wildly superior plan of God's for the very very short-lived and fleeting feeling of fitting in. Sound familiar?

What really does and should excite me about this is that the end result of me handing over the keys of my life and the plan for that customized life to God is not a life cluttered with "stuff." It is a rich life full of impact, purpose, meaningful relationships, and a lasting legacy of hope and grace. And while this might not be enough to land any of us on the cover of *Time Magazine* for Person of the Year, it very well should result in hearing "well done thou good and faithful servant." What could be better than hearing this from the Creator of the universe when our time on Earth has come to an end? But as it should be, the theme for me and all of us throughout this book is *time is of the essence*. If I take my car to get customized at the shop, they will ask many questions but two of the more pertinent ones will be: how long do I have to work on this and how much do you have to spend? The more time and resources I give them, the better the end result. The more of my life I offer God and if I go all-in with my commitment of energy to letting Him customize my life as He has planned, the better and richer my life can be.

9

SMOOTHIE KING

IN OUR FAMILY, THE consensus for a meal is sometimes a smoothie. We all find our desired flavor out of the available menu choices. We generally choose this on a hot day when we want a little pick-me-up or after some physical activity. There is usually an option to add small amounts of extra health centric ingredients to boost our desired benefit—maybe a little more protein or immune booster or energy jolt. It is, in a sense, an afterthought—albeit a refreshing one in the moment—but often sprinkled in between an otherwise ad hoc eating pattern that can leave us drained and unenergized. Then there is the diet of the world-class athlete set on not only competing but excelling amongst a sea of other elite athletes. They, in this quest to dominate, often hire a team of nutritionists, chefs, and doctors to customize a diet regimen (amongst other things) that specifically account for them: their

God's Plan

sport, body type, and specific goals. In other words, in this quest to reach otherwise unreachable places, they give up full control of the plan by which they get there.

This to me in many ways represents the choice in front of all of us. I can live my life, in full control of the plan but occasionally, as an afterthought, pray and ask God for a little boost of help to my committed to plan. And just like with the smoothie, predictably, when our plans fall flat or leave us feeling unfulfilled, it is tempting for to default to asking "where was God?" The truth is He was exactly where I put Him – in a small box as an afterthought and hopeful insurance policy to my plan. Conversely, when I give up full control of my plans, and allow the ultimate life doctor, nutritionist, and chef in God to leverage the unique talents He's gifted me with and shape both the plan and steps needed to reach the fully envisioned and customized life plan He has for me, really good things happen. Very few of us will ever have the skills or resources necessary to be an elite, world champion athlete. However, not one of us is ineligible to get 100 percent of everything God has to offer for His life plan for us. Yet somehow, there are many times throughout my life that I had a difficult time relinquishing control in order for Him to do His absolute best work in my life.

Fear of the unknown is a powerful and constant obstacle in my quest to live a God-anchored life.

While I know my plans fall short of my expectations, before I start, I convince myself that I get to control the inputs and thus the outputs. But as Pastor Gregg Matte frequently says, "There is nothing more empty or crushing than finding out that you climbed the ladder of life that was leaned against the wrong wall." When I read testimonies from the early stages of these top athletes' dietary journeys, the early stages are the toughest. Old habits and tendencies must be unlearned and initially, it often seems that performance and outcomes are actually getting worse. In a world increasingly consumed by immediacy and a constant stream of feel-good superficial emotions, the initial process adds to the fear and impulse to abandon the plan.

It is always comical (seems that these are somehow more enjoyable to read about than experience) to read the commentary of the transitional pain points these athletes have. The late-night binge eating and fast-food trips are replaced by careful pre-planned meals and caloric intake. This would be a jolt for anyone and take time to process and change. This feels similar to my spiritual growth at different times, but especially in this most recent season where I have more intentionally moved toward complete surrender to Him and a plan that often does not conform to any of the "norms" of this world. It takes work to reconfigure my day and thought pattern to be in communication with

God and be listening for how He wants to work in and through me.

There is an interesting place all of these athletes reach in the quest to reach their maximum performance. There is a specific moment when they realize that not only have they begun to perform and feel better, but the same activities and dietary changes that were initially so hard to conform to have now, in fact, become a very natural and key part of who they are and what they do. Those things they enjoyed eating and doing before have in fact become so incompatible with their new goals and lifestyle that they are almost disgusted that they ever did or ate them to begin with. With age and growth, I am hopefully in better alignment with what God has specifically designed for me in His plan and less intrigued by the things that I used to follow as part of my plan.

The journey never ends for athletes. They evolve in their career thus necessitating constant monitoring and adjusting. The same set of choices that faced them early in their transformation will always exist. They frequently meet with the experts that created the plan and adjust it as required. Somehow, I want to hit a magical plateau here on Earth where I'm on cruise control with all necessary God-planned ingredients in place. But God knows me and all of us too well. We do not operate well on cruise control and often abandon

God in these moments. Communication must be constant, and God craves and desires a relationship with each of us that has communication as a central theme. Life stages bring new challenges, people, and situations that require me to be in constant communion with God so I can make necessary adjustments to reach my full potential in each of these phases.

It turns out that in life, I can still enjoy the smoothie with that extra shot of protein and make good exercise and diet choices. However, when it comes to the larger, all-encompassing life I have been gifted with, there is no mixing my plan and God's plan if my true desire is to be as fulfilled and impactful as God intended. Sure, we can all try our best to customize and mix and match our plans with God's plans, but I sometimes envision sitting with God in heaven rewatching film on our lives (scary thought I know) with Him offering up the full playbook and things He had designed to be part of our lives. My new purpose, while often not well executed, is to try to minimize the size of the gap between these two pieces of film at the end, to make the life I have lived on Earth be as close as possible to the one God wants me to. What will be your new life purpose under His plan?

10

BUSINESS PLAN REWRITE

THERE ARE NUMEROUS STORIES of God's influence in the redirection of someone's life—both in and outside of the Bible. And there is perhaps no more succinct and noted story than that of Zacchaeus (Matthew 19), who, as kids we sang, "was a wee little man." He was doing well for himself as the chief tax collector, albeit not exactly honest and honorable. Like everyone in that moment, he was caught up in the Jesus fervor, and he simply wanted a glimpse to see what all the fuss was about. Being vertically challenged, climbing up into a sycamore tree was the only way his glimpse was possible. But what began as a quick glance escalated into a total life and game changer—the complete rewriting of Zacchaeus's life business plan. One minute he's simply gazing and probably contemplating what tax collecting duties he would be resuming the rest of the day, and the next minute Jesus zeros in on him.

"Let's go right now, Zach—I must go to your house." Even as the crowd starts to react and whisper, what we are blessed to observe is nothing short of one of the most dramatic turnaround stories we will find. Not only does Zacchaeus enthusiastically welcome Jesus into his home, but he immediately changes course from his life plan to a new life under God's direction. In his transition, I see and feel what I am calling the 3 Cs.

First, in Zacchaeus we find a real curiosity. This story, while succinct, does leave out some of the backstory, juicy emotions, and details that Hallmark movies have conditioned all of us to think we must have. However, we know enough to know that his curiosity was piqued—piqued enough to stop his day, show up, and even climb up in a tree to get a better view. One of the real dangers for me, and I presume all of us living in today's world, is I become so focused and caught up in the noise around me and executing my plans for life that I lack the most basic, necessary level of curiosity to see what Jesus is potentially orchestrating in my life. Think about the thousands of people Jesus walked by during His time on Earth and the relatively few we see Him note as stopping and engaging with. He seems to have a heightened sensitivity to those ready to engage Him. Without that tree climbing moment, Zacchaeus never makes an appearance in the Bible—simply another wealthy man who leaves this earth quietly and unnoted.

Next, through that initial curiosity we find conviction. By making the effort to find and see Jesus, Zacchaeus invites Jesus into his world. We don't read or see any lengthy stream of consciousness as he's climbing the tree, but whatever he's thinking the minute, Jesus points and says, "Let's go Zach—we have to talk—time to change your life." Zacchaeus is all in and welcomes Jesus into his world. It's safe to say from other stories in the Bible, given the gift of free will that we all receive, this response is never a foregone conclusion. What I also appreciate from this narrative is that we do not even get a window into the conversation that occurred inside of Zacchaeus's home. I sometimes incorrectly associate "conviction" with this really negative and intense Jesus-sponsored guilt trip. However, as I mature and age, I find what life-altering conviction really looks like for me is merely Jesus kindly but intentionally holding up a mirror that simply reveals the things He knows I need to change in order to experience the fullest life possible according to His perfect plan. This gentle but loving approach should leave me encouraged, not discouraged, hopeful, not hopeless.

Finally, out of this home visit from Jesus and reflective-mirror exercise, we see Zacchaeus emerge changed. That is the final C. He does not walk out and declare, "Wow, Jesus, you've given me so many good ideas to think about. I can't wait to process this and make some tweaks to my life." No, it's an immediate "I'm in... all in." What's tragic about the way I tend to process God's intent and plan for my life is that I want to push it through the same analytical rigor that I would weigh any other idea or thought in life. That's a problem because it almost guarantees I am straddling some fence between my plan and His. I want to hold onto the notion that there are somehow redemptive qualities about my selfish and flawed plan. And as we know with clean water and mud, the minute I try to drop in a little of my plan, I have immediately compromised all of His. Jesus did not mince words about this in Revelation 3:16—he calls this "lukewarm" and says he has no interest in coauthoring life plans with us. He needs and wants us to be changed—completely changed.

It seems poetic that a man explicitly noted for his small stature, enjoys the amazing distinction of a giant faith in Jesus and a completely new plan for his life. What started as a quick glance, permanently changed his entire approach. It's impossible as a six-year-old singing the infamous Zacchaeus song to grasp the enormity of what transpired in these ten verses in Matthew 19. Thankfully, as an adult with some life under my belt, it is equally impossible to miss the application opportunity. Jesus will never force His plan on me, but when I make myself available, invite Him completely in, and get to work in total alignment with what He has, then I am blessed with the chance to immediately redirect my path and find new opportunities and blessings otherwise never touched.

11

ASYMMETRIC

WHEN IT COMES TO real estate and design, I am wired to love symmetry. I like rooms and spaces to feel balanced. If there is something on one side, I generally like to see something of equal mass, scale, and shape on the other side. For whatever reason this look puts my mind at ease when I walk into a space. As I think about it, that is often the way I think we all tend to approach life and relationships. We naturally crave equally weighted balances and want to feel there is an equitable exchange. When we find we are with people or in situations that are unbalanced for too long, we can get anxious, irritated, and feel taken advantage of. However, when it comes to my approach to life and balancing my plan against God's, He calls us to enjoy the most asymmetric and unbalanced approach ever. There is only one plan and it's His—anything resembling "balance" in that regard is "anything but." It

God's Plan

sounds so simple, but striving for such perfect imbalance is a daily commitment on my part that requires several ingredients.

First, what is not and cannot be out of balance in this one-sided plan is the way I engage in communication with Jesus. Because His plan is often unfamiliar and nothing like the world's plans, it means I must be in a constant dialogue with Jesus to stay on track. I must be focused enough to express my heart through prayer, be sensitive enough to hear His often-quiet voice in the Bible and be aware enough to pick up on the cues He sends through other people. Ironically, it is all too easy for me to get out of balance in these areas. The human default setting is unfortunately one of self-sufficiency, passivity, and a lot of I'll-call-you-if-I-need-you. But whenever I find myself in the healthy rhythm of communication with the Author of the plan for my life, while the outcomes and outputs may look nothing like I envisioned, the peace I'm able to experience in trusting I'm in alignment with Him is life-giving.

Second, I find that I must become comfortable living out a life that throws the world for a loop. God is going to ask of me things that defy and run against what the world is coaching and encouraging me and all of us to do. The bulk of the plan He has reserved for me involves loving like He loved and serving like He served. So, this very same world that will sometimes head scratch at what I am up to is also the single biggest benefactor of His plan. However, I have to be okay living inside this tension. Often this tension involves the balance between love and truth. The world is a hot mess, living intentionally without God in it, and thus struggling to define love and truth without Him to anchor these foundational beliefs. Chaos is the end result. When I am able to enter people's lives under God's complete direction, bound by His truth and presented in His love, the one-sided approach should be an immediate breath of fresh air for a world gasping for some semblance of peace and joy.

Finally, I am learning to embrace the seemingly unbalanced beauty of working underneath the God Operating System. When I conform to His direction for my life, then the more dialed into that plan I become and the more I find that there is no plan that offers me more fulfillment and completeness than His. He understands my needs and deepest desires even better than I do and knows that there are amazing and inexplicable outcomes and feelings of complete fulfillment and peace that can only be unearthed by my complete adherence to what He is mapping out. I am drawn to the immediacy and the short-lived here and now, but it is these distracting and often all-consuming pursuits from my plan which are actually the

God's Plan

most counterproductive to who and what I know I need to become.

There are times when I can be almost OCD about the symmetry (or lack thereof) that I might see in a room. It is almost calming to see this sense of balance achieved. Wouldn't it be great for me and all of us to have that same level of urgency or discomfort when we find our own lives sliding away from God's direction for us and into the comfortable ruts that are destined for nowhere?

12

HOLY TAP-OUT

THE MODERN-DAY VERSION OF gladiators is ultimate fighting that happens inside of an eight-sided cage appropriately termed the octagon. In this near fight-to-the-death style of fighting where phenomenal athletes exchange blows nothing short of violent, there are several ways a fight can end before its scheduled conclusion. None of these premature ends to a fight are particularly pleasant for the fighter on the losing end of the match. But one of the ways this end can happen is a tap out where one of the fighters puts the other fighters head, arm, leg, or whatever they can gain full control of into such a compromised (and what always appears to be unbelievably painful) position, that the defeated fighter merely taps their hand in a visible way. This small gesture makes a huge fight-ending signal: "I'm done here—I've been beaten and fully submit to my opponent. I'm surrendering to them." For these

God's Plan

fighters, this moment is one I imagine they dread the most—visibly admitting they've been outmatched. However, I can make a case that when it comes to the decision each of us must make as it relates to the plan we live out for our lives, our willingness to acknowledge and embrace what I affectionately call the holy tap out sooner rather than later completely and visibly acknowledges our complete submission to God's plan for each of us. The result: the sooner we can get to work on His plan.

It turns out God knows something about ultimate fighting. In Genesis 32, we find the somewhat unexpected depiction of God wrestling with Jacob. Jacob, for most of his life until this defining moment, seems to have been on the my-life-my-plan trajectory. Literally from birth where he was hustling to get an edge over his twin brother Esau, he'd been scheming and living pretty much how he wanted. In many ways it was working out, but it was also coming with increased collateral damage in terms of relationships. But on this one night, he literally picked a fight with God and had his tap out moment. God could have ended it before it started, but He let it play out. The end result was a submitted Jacob. Out of that place of submission, God could do amazing things—it is not every day God changes someone's name on the spot to what became one of the most important names in history: Israel.

So, what about me and what about you? Where are we in the critical submission process as it relates to the plan we use for our lives? As we saw with Jacob, anything short of complete tap out leaves us in an agonizing struggle. God is persistent and available but always gracious and honoring of the gift of free will. He will wait as long as it takes, but the longer it takes me to take the massive step forward and signal that I am 100 percent in alignment with where and how He wants me to proceed in life, the higher the opportunity costs are for me. Just look at Jacob. He lied to his dad, stole from his brother, and had the toughest father-in-law interaction I've ever heard of. While He was a profoundly changed person after this holy wrestling match, he still had to contend and live with all the self-inflicted baggage.

There is a silver lining in the struggle that hopefully results sooner rather than later in this God-organized tap out. It is the struggle for Jacob and most of us that strengthens and cements our conviction and resulting surrender. When I have battled with my human tendencies to want control and the surrender God seeks, I realize both the complete inadequacies of my efforts and the sheer immenseness of God's endless capacity to fill in all my gaps. As a result, my faith in God grows by leaps and bounds. With each chapter of life living in this truth, I discover that if I can learn from previous chapters, I am more anxious if not excited to quickly tap out to everything God has for me.

13

NO CHEATING

ONE OF THE MORE enjoyable journeys I have been able to observe from a distance is seeing my wife take on the role of health coach to other women. She has been able to apply both formal training and God-given people-centric passions and giftings to help encourage women of all ages and stages find a new life through healthier eating and exercise. In observing this process, I've come to appreciate and recognize some similar dynamics and parallels between my life and plan. In a sense, each of these people Stacey gets the privilege to work with comes because they recognize their health plan isn't working. The truth is, the number of people that reach near nirvana levels of health and wellness, even under her coaching and oversight, is still relatively low. I can zero in on a couple of key components that seem to be required for success on this health journey that are infinitely more important on life's journey.

The first thing that has to occur on this health journey Stacey takes people on is a pretty thorough and immediate inventory of the pantry and general habits. While everyone is there because of the desire to improve their health, there is typically an eye-opening moment when they are asked to take several key measurements of their body to establish a baseline to grade future improvements against. This is never meant to shame anyone but become a source of encouragement as they progress down a road of better outcomes. There is a similar exercise I must start with, monitor, and be accountable for in my spiritual journey and specific efforts to align with God's plan. When I live in a confusing place of denial, where I want "better" but refuse to acknowledge the "need" I have, I forfeit the chance to improve.

The second thing I have observed from this exercise is the need to simply take steps forward to improve habits which become foundational to a completely new and sustainable way for healthier living. If I am not careful, I can become paralyzed in my efforts to shift from my plan to one completely focused on God's best for me. I can create quite impressive sounding reasons for waiting until I have several things lined up. This invariably leads to just a continuation of the path I have been on—the one that is failing most days and leaving me breathless and exhausted. The real danger

No Cheating

for Stacey's clients and me in this moment is that I have now been made keenly aware of my plan's significant deficits and staying the course is only assured to come with even more crushing pain and pressure knowing there is a better option.

Finally, in this lifelong quest for "better" both for Stacey's clients and me, there is the necessary realization that the pathway to somewhere far more fulfilling and lasting will not be easy. The habits and things that resulted in her clients and me arriving at a place we desperately want to get out of also became comfortable and are not easy to shift away from. But just as Stacey serves from a place of grace, where a bad day does not mean all previous efforts are negated, God also patiently affords us the daily opportunity to regroup, recenter on Him and push ahead with fresh perspective and renewed hope in the plan He's designed for us. So, while there is no cheating or hybrid path that will ever be sponsored by Him—it's simply incompatible—He is incredibly loving in His stewardship of both our hearts and work in and through our lives.

It is lifegiving for me to inhale the secondhand feedback from one of Stacey's clients months and years after working with her, gushing about how profoundly better her and even her family's lives have been impacted by the dietary and exercise changes they have made. I would never want to take away from these powerful moments, but they do somehow pale in comparison to life that shifts away from the fruitless efforts of a self-crafted plan to one that is in full alignment with God's will and plan. He does not allow for cheating or partial implementation, but He is always standing by, full of all the grace, direction, and coaching needed for us to find our way into the most successful and fulfilling outcomes possible. If someone simply making a couple of key lifestyle changes can come to the end of this process and comment, "I did not think it was possible to feel this good," how much greater and more significant is the final statement we can and should be able to make at the end of a life diligently lived seeking only God's plan?

14

GOD CARES SO MUCH

OUR FAMILY WAS FORTUNATE to take a once in a lifetime trip to Israel and see so many of the locations that we had all read about and studied in our Bibles for years. Each night at dinner, the group from our church we were with would just sit and relish reliving the experiences, even struggling to begin to pick any favorites. On the final night, after a week packed with so many impactful moments and sites, we gathered together for one more dinner in Jerusalem. One of the pastors asked people to stand up and share what they had learned during that week. Adults and children took turns sharing; many of the testimonies were personal and moving. Finally, toward the end, a young girl stood up and came to the front. We were all expecting something completely cute, but not necessarily profound. However, she surprised us all by expressing perhaps the most poignant message we had heard. She said, "I learned this week that God cares... I mean He really cares." She went on to share that everything we saw was overwhelming evidence that God really cares about this world and each of us in it. And as I fully processed this message through the context and lens of my life and comfort level in allowing God to fully control it, it was freeing and enlightening.

While not everyone was fortunate to grow up with the parental experience my brother and I had, I am grateful we did. I was gifted from the beginning with fully committed Christian parents. They devoted efforts and energy that went into creating an environment that was conducive to our development, discipline, and eventual launch into life. They did verbalize that they cared deeply for us, but it was the actions they took that spoke the loudest. And because of that care, in many ways my brother and I willingly relinquished control of our "plans" those first eighteen years to listen to and be coached by them. Had they given us reasons to mistrust them and question their true intent, it would have been difficult, if not impossible, to embrace or follow their advice and direction. Frankly, I don't even want to stop and think where I would be today without their caring and stabilizing force behind us.

Unfortunately for many in today's world, this is unfamiliar. But sitting there on a beautiful and peaceful evening in Jerusalem reminded me and everyone there that there is a universal and readily available Father whose level of care from the beginning remains unmatched for everyone. As we sat and recounted story after story from the week, we could feel the palpable level of deep rooted, unchanging care He has for each human. The stories in the Bible had come to life for each of us in a vivid reminder that they weren't Hollywood-created dramatic moments, but historically accurate realities of the Christian faith. Perhaps nowhere was this more evident than retracing the final steps Jesus took before He died for all of mankind in the most notable act of care to ever happen.

Hearing this simple message that I could not in any way refute just made me realize that if God cares this deeply for me and everyone around me, then there simply is no other appropriate response than to completely trust God's plan for my life with His wildly capable and masterful hands. Now, we all know these amazing and unique mountain top experiences do pass and the emotion I felt at that moment did subside. Since then, first thing in the morning when I am doing my quiet time and asking God what He wants to say through the Bible, I try to remind myself of that care He has, recommit to live that day for Him, and ask for His forgiveness where I am stubbornly holding on to things I know are getting in the way

God's Plan

of His perfect plans for me. Not easy—but there is something refreshing about always being able to come back to this simple but profound truth: "He cares... He really really cares." Can you hear Him whispering this to you, too?

15

DON'T BENCH GOD

I WAS THAT GUY from the 1990s—the one who spent my teen years during this decade trying very unsuccessfully to replicate just a fraction of the basketball success I was watching play out on the court by the iconic Michael Jordan. He was mesmerizing to watch and defined a sport and apparel empire forever. Just imagine, as inconceivable as it is, his coaches during that moment had decided to bench him—somehow despite his ability to transform the team and everyone around him into something historically good, the coach knew better. Had that happened, the Chicago Bulls would never win six championships, many of the players around him would be never heard of, and basketball as we know likely would not look the same. Although Michael was physically gifted beyond our wildest basketball dreams, he was no god. But we serve an incredibly and infinitely more talented God.

God's Plan

However, He has gifted you and me with freewill and in that space we can "bench" God in our lives. As silly as it is to think about Coach Phil Jackson telling Michael to sit on the bench because he's got a better plan, it's somehow even more perplexing to think about my occasional (and unfortunately at times frequent) tendency to do just that with God and His plan for my life.

Michael Jordan elevated everyone else's game. He pulled out of players and coaches talents and skills that would have gone otherwise unnoticed and, even perhaps, undiscovered at all. Even when he was not hitting the game-winning shot, his mere presence on the court created game winning shot opportunities for others. Imagine for a second a God with infinitely more capabilities than MJ and without the harsh edge. When I allow God off the bench and into my life—all of it—I find that I become a version of myself that is far better and more capable. The bonus of this faith-building exercise seems to be that others around me take notice and also want to be and become better. However, unfortunately, the opposite is true. There was a season when Jordan took a hiatus to pursue a short-lived career attempting to play major league base-ball. His batting average was not the only thing that suffered. The Chicago Bulls he left behind were unable to win a championship. It was, for the most part, the same talented group and they did play well for a while. However, without his presence, over time the giant hole he left behind made it quickly clear this group would flounder. I am the same and I suspect everyone reading this is too. Pull God and my day-to-day interaction with Him out of my life, and it does not take long for there to be fraying on the edges and far worse. Whatever view of talent that I possess withers without Him invited into my world to help breathe life into my interactions and activities.

Statistics do not always translate into wins. Scotty Pippen, largely considered to be Michael Jordan's most important teammate for most his career, racked up his most impressive statistical season the year MJ played baseball. He did the absolute best he could to fill the enormous gap that was there; but, at the end of the day, those stats still left him short when it came to winning a championship. There are countless players—extremely good ones—who enjoy impressive statistical records and feats but ultimately lack respect and notoriety because it simply never translated into a career marked by any championships. I would never claim that someone like Jordan cures all professional basketball woes, but I will readily claim that keeping God actively engaged and the driving force behind the plans we operate under in life can and should be game changing. Statistical chasing in life means that if

God's Plan

I am not careful, I am very susceptible to the pursuit of various accolades, which in and of themselves are not inherently bad. However, there is a huge difference in me following a fully God-sponsored plan that results in me making $100M to advance Kingdom work and me kicking and scratching my way to $100M and having very little to show for it other than relational carnage scattered along the way and no purpose.

Michael Jordan was a force of nature and asserted himself to almost will his team to come along. He was often frustrated that his teammates could not keep pace or did not possess his level of skill. That's the truly beautiful thing I find about keeping God in the game of our lives. His talent and skill are completely unmatched and I can only imagine how many times a day He is justified to look at me and just shake His head and lose His mind: "There Mike goes again—he reacted poorly to that or wasn't patient enough there or lacked trust in Me." Thankfully, this is not His approach at all. He's everything I need to be much more of: patient, loving, kind, and understanding. But in that, He also has plans and expectations for where He wants to take me that are infinitely higher than what I can imagine. He will correct, teach, and coach me along the way. But for that to work, I have to daily invite Him into my world and make sure I do not end up allowing my life to fall short of His ultimate design

Don't Bench God

for me because I elect to use my free will to keep Him on the bench. Have you been giving God too much bench time in your own life?

16

LEAD-OUT RIDER

THERE WAS A MOMENT in the early 2000s when I became intrigued by the world of cycling, particularly the Tour de France, and started dabbling (I use that term loosely) in it myself to supplement my running. It was challenging and far more technical than I remembered the last time I messed around on a bike as a child. But watching this exhausting three-week race across Europe, artfully captured by NBC every summer, I discovered it was in fact full of drama, strategy, and tactics. And amazingly, entire teams were structured and built largely around one rider who was deemed to have the best overall chance to win the entire race. There is perhaps no higher level of sacrifice exemplified than that of the lead-out rider. Their job is to spend much of the ride leading the pack, but specifically guiding the team's main rider through the course, potentially in close quarters with other riders, for the sole purpose of delivering them safely to the end of the race in the optimal position to win that day's race stage. I'm always amazed at this play out as they empty themselves and fade into the pack at the very end, all for the singular purpose of lifting someone else up. God is so much more for us than a lead-out rider, but I see parallels worth noting that highlight my profound need for these lead-out qualities in my life.

One of the first things that I noticed among these high-performing cycling teams is the level of communication. As I was getting familiarized with this new world of cycling on my own starter road bike, I went on a couple of group rides—well kind of group rides until I couldn't keep up. It was a little nerve racking realizing how close these guys rode together and at relatively fast speeds. I quickly discovered through intense observations that at high speeds, there isn't always a lot of chatting but rather very quick hand signals that are passed from the front of the pack to the back to alert other riders of various things to watch out for: something only the lead-out rider can see. The teams on the Tour de France elevate their communication to a much higher level but the premise remains the same. For the designated rider to win the stage of the race that day, they must be in constant communication with that lead-out rider and their team. Every once in a while, you could sense that a team was having a breakdown in communication and the results were not good. For me to feel good about the plan God has for me, I must be in constant communication with Him. It is far easier to make small adjustments based on small inputs than risk crashing or getting off course completely.

The next thing I have noticed is the result of repeated quality communication is the level of trust the top rider has in his lead-out rider. The peloton, or what the cycling novice in me learned is the lightning-fast massive pile of riders riding together, is the source of many race-ending moments for teams as crashes are always a risk and almost never small. The lead-out rider must navigate safely through the mass of only-inches-from-each-other riders over and over. In some ways the more precarious the position, the more important it is for him to follow closely. However, even in the seemingly clear moments, there is an equally important role of pace setting, refueling, and other managed efforts that ultimately lead to the best possible end result. So, too, do I find myself in constant need to tuck in close each day to what God has for me. Sometimes, in the immediate moment, a day can look fruitless or even unproductive. But, as I continue to grow and mature, when I am confident that I have leaned my full weight into what He has, then I can also grow in my confidence that God, seeing the entire picture I never can or will, has taken

God's Plan

me through day, moment, or season thus positioning for me something He has further down the road.

The one beautiful difference between God as my "lead-out" is that He never leaves or fades any part. He was there from the beginning, right in the middle, and will be at the end and into eternity. However, in the western world, and with my type-A personality, what I do find I have to constantly be refining and redefining is understanding and even accepting what "stage wins" look like. The world around us is less than helpful in wanting to help inform what "wins" looks like. If Steve Jobs, in all his incredible successes and wealth, can lay on his death bed questioning all of that in much the same way Solomon did in Ecclesiastes, then it probably means one of the biggest challenges you and I can expect to face and continue to confront is how to view success along this journey of following God's perfect plan for our lives. It all starts and ends with my relationships. When my vertical relationship with God is off, my horizontal relationships with people soon follow, and no other worldly success can redeem or make up for those. But when I am able to let the ultimate lead-out rider of my life guide me, and I tuck in close behind Him, good things start to happen.

17

BRAGGING RIGHTS

JESUS'S MINISTRY ON EARTH was three short years, but no one before or since has ever accomplished more for the human race than He did. Once it started, He was an unstoppable force. Everything He did and said was profoundly different than anything or anyone else. His care, depth, and knowledge were unmatched. He used physical healing to highlight and expose our much deeper need for Him and His guiding hand in our lives. There are twenty-three of these healings recorded in the Bible, but the Bible makes vague reference to countless more that went unrecorded as He went all over the countryside. What jumps out to me is the aftermath from these healings. I see the same basic pattern. Someone was in a desperate situation that, absent Jesus's intervention, was likely headed for an early death following a life of complete misery and a near-invisible existence. Once they received their sight back or could walk, they immediately left and were forever changed. Not even Jesus, sometimes instructing them to stay quiet about it, could taper their unbridled enthusiasm to share and, dare I say, brag on Jesus. What I don't see any evidence of in any of these accounts is of people saying anything to the effect: "Well to be honest, it was only a matter of time. I've done a lot of things, and my hard work finally paid off when Jesus showed up." As I mature and commit daily to a life under the full control of God's plan, I then get to see the undeserved fruits of this life, which in turn offers me the chance to merely reflect my light back to the source and brag on God.

First, in these healings, I see people who have a completely objective view of their pre-Jesus life. Society has marginalized them almost completely out of existence, and they have nothing outside of the scraps that might get thrown their way. Their entire state of existence is so utterly desperate that Jesus kindly and wisely offers to restore their physical ailments only as a symbolic reference to the real work going on in their soul. While perhaps this is likely not fully comprehended in the moment, it seems to bring about a universal and enthusiastic response from each of them. My fear for me and many of us who have grown up without anything close to this complete level of desperation is that it becomes, in some ways, challenging to receive the gift of a transformed new life and plan with the right mindset. I remember recently spending a week with our oldest daughter at JH Ranch in Northern California. It was a powerful week, and each day was capped off with an evening service that began with worship. On one of the first nights, the lead worship leader challenged everyone there, who already felt sold out to the moment, to ask themselves if each of us was really as desperate for Jesus as we needed to be. The danger and risk of not coming to this realization that these down-and-out people in the Bible did, is that, as God works in and through me, I potentially can make the mistake of misdirecting any credit for the work He's doing to myself.

Second, and perhaps because of the recognition of the starting point, these people cannot help but shout to anyone who will listen about what happened. The religious leaders were already frustrated with this Messiah Jesus and were trying to reconcile the mounting stories of miracles and transformed lives against centuries of closely held traditions and views. The people, recently given a completely new life trajectory, kept it simple. In John 9, it is almost comical as these religious leaders question a recently healed blind man and try to trip him up and make claims about Jesus. He will not come off his story and in a sense says, "Hey, I'm not quite sure where you're going with this but all I know

God's Plan

is I was blind and after encountering Jesus, I can see."
There is an infectious joy that slips through the words
and one can only imagine that as these formerly belea-
guered people returned to their respective communi-
ties completely changed physically, what ultimately
drew others to them was an entirely new outlook on
life and perhaps, most importantly, their starting to
reflect the Source of all this change. I would almost
call this holy bragging; they wanted everyone to hear
about this Jesus who had changed everything. And it
is from this place that they undoubtedly had tremendous impact. I must resist the urge to assign any level
of credit to myself from the things Jesus has done and
will do in and through me. When I do, I lower the
volume of His message, diminish the power behind it,
and likely limit the reach of how and where God wants
to use me through His plan to reach others.

Finally, we see no evidence that any one of these
people ended up anywhere close to where Jesus origi-
nally found them. Can you imagine how crazy it would
read in the Bible if it said, "And returning the next day
to where Jesus had discovered him, the formerly blind
man met with Jesus to discuss and agree on a new life
that mixed and matched his former life of begging
with his newfound sight. With a little ingenuity, he
was able to modestly improve his previously dismal
existence." It seems to be nothing like that. Jesus was

the embodiment of new and seems to always breathe a completely different existence into these lives, "I know it's been tough, but it's go time now and because of where you've been and what I've done, I need you to go turn your community upside down. Share with them what I've done for you so they can experience it to." I need to read, receive, and respond to this simple message in my life.

In some ways, the dramatic conversion and experience of these various "down and outs" makes it feel simpler to respond to. But the older I get, the more I appreciate the eternal simplicity and relevancy of the truths captured in these healing stories. These people suddenly got the ultimate life plan redirect—from a dead end to the end zone in one fell swoop. And from then on, there was no reason to follow any other plan except the one Jesus offered and no way to give credit to anyone else but Him. Are you letting God get the credit for the things He has done in your life?

18

JOINT OPERATION

WHEN THE UNITED STATES puts its full weight behind a military operation, and wants to ensure complete dominance and success, they execute a comprehensive plan or joint operation that utilizes all the branches of the military (Army, Navy, Marines, and Air Force) and each of their unique capabilities. While each of these branches has their specific mission, it is interconnected to and dependent on the other branches' ability to also execute their respective mission as part of one ultimate plan. To say this is "not easy" is an understatement, but it is critical for the successful outcomes of military operations. In the last four to five years of marriage, I come to view marriage through this lens and its vital and critical role in God's plan for my life. If I'm not careful, I can start to treat it like us being two roommates as my wife Stacey will occasionally warn us against. Under that scenario, the mantra is: let's just

work together best we can, keep it civil, leverage and
pool resources, and see if we can somehow survive to
the end. But I have been convicted, challenged, and
inspired lately to want and desire more from myself
and for my marriage to Stacey than that. Just like
the Army or Navy, neither could ever accomplish
anything on their own like they could when working
in tandem, I believe more than ever that God's plan
for me is intertwined with Stacey's and that He has
called us to be on mission together.

This is not in any way intended to downplay those
called to singlehood, but for many of us marriage is a
gift that is an integral part of our day-to-day lives, so it
seems warranted to park here for a minute and explore
it in the context of God's plan. It is impossible for me
to talk about God's plan for my life without me wrap-
ping that around Stacey, her gifts, passions, and God's
plan for her. Kevin Phillips and Mark Schatzman,
on *Kevin's Kingdom Citizen* podcast on Kingdom
Marriage, do a deep dive into the need for marriage
to be the ultimate reflection of Jesus and for couples
to be purposeful with their joint operation together.
In other words, it becomes the interconnectedness of
a committed marriage between a man and a woman
that offers the world the most complete picture of
God and has the best opportunity to accomplish the
most for Him. Just like with the military, the critical

Joint Operation

importance of the roles and plans God has for each of us individually, are not ignored; but they are always taken into the context of the larger plan He has for both of us working hand in hand.

The enemy recognizes the tremendous power of a family unit working in tandem and on mission for God. He will do almost anything to break apart families and marriages, and in doing so have devastating impact on God's intended plan for both individuals and couples. In the military, one of the most dreaded moments in a joint operation is called "friendly fire." It is the moment when a stray missile from a jet, intended to protect troops on the ground, inadvertently actually strikes the same group. The very tools meant to support the other and create a distinct advantage on the battlefield suddenly become the enemy from within. If Stacey and I are not extremely intentional about our relationship with God and then with each other, I can slip off course and suddenly be at odds with her. It might not have the immediate impact of the "friendly fire" incident, but it is no less dangerous and at a minimum ensures that the individual and intertwined plans God has set out for us have paused, if not regressed. Unfortunately for me, I know when I feel the "pressure of life" it is often Stacey and my family who endure the least impressive version of me. While I have hopefully become quick at recognizing these moments and resetting through sincere confession, my goal remains to have these friction points of unnecessary "friendly fire" become less and less frequent.

For Stacey and me, our joint operation when working at its best is all the fruits of the spirit—love, joy, peace, patience, kindness, goodness, faithfulness, gentleness, and self-control—on display for others to see. We have always attempted to be a safe place for people to feel welcomed and loved. It has been amazing to embrace and grow in this over the years and try to love the way Jesus would and does. We have been able to learn from and invest in other couples, parents, and children. It is not that we could not have done that in our God-honoring singleness; but, as a team on mission together, we are simply able to be part of a larger plan. And an interesting thing has happened for each of us. As we continue to pursue growth through God in our marriage, both of us would say that God has in turn enhanced our individual talents and plans way beyond what we were otherwise capable of. The way Stacey supported me through business school, professional peaks and valleys, and even in this crazy thing called "writing" has been powerful and life-giving. Hopefully in the same way, I have tried (although it is nearly impossible to match the amazing support of this former cheerleader) to help encourage and lift her

Joint Operation

and limitless potential and endless care and love for others to new heights.

It is incredibly challenging to coordinate the efforts of the Navy, Marine, Army, and Air Force to accomplish a unified mission, but the stakes and costs are too high not to make every effort align in these distinct groups. The world today desperately needs to see, feel, and touch flourishing marriages with husbands and wives so in tune with their Creator and aligned with each other, that there are multiple levels of concentric circles within their community feeding off their infectious effort. We all know this truth, but people are always watching. I never want to do anything for show or fear, but it should in fact fuel me to be better and use our marriage as an opportunity to be a beacon of Christ-reflected light for others to be drawn to.

19

REACH AND PULL

"Therefore encourage one another and build one another up, just as you are doing."

I Thessalonians 5:11

WHEN I THINK ABOUT my life falling into the track and the plan God designed, I cannot fathom it happening for any of us without a steady diet of others in our lives. God has used countless people throughout my life—different people for different seasons—who have sharpened me, challenged me, supported me, and stretched and pulled me along and supported His plan for my life. And hopefully my life has been woven in and out of others in the same way. In its simplest form, I find I always want to be reaching out to mentor types, or those men and married couples who are further down the road of life and are living in the same ways I aspire to. At the same time, I love looking for ways to simultaneously extend my hand of experience to those coming behind me. Somewhere in between both of those groups is a special group of peers who reach and pull each other through the phases of life. In this world of God's economy, He utilizes the interconnectedness of our lives to others in much the same way the intertwined roots of giant redwood trees to aid in their growth and resistance to the elements.

One of the things I admire more and more about mentor-type people that I learn and grow the most from is their humility and desire for improvement. It is from this place of authenticity and vulnerability that I am drawn into. They listen, they care, and they speak the truth I need to hear. It is direct without being condemning. It is probing without being nosey. They invest in me and earn the right to help pull me back into alignment to where God wants me going. These are the people that call or text right at the moment I am struggling with something. I have learned that these wise and available God-ordained sherpas of sorts must be reached for. Their resource will sit there untapped if I am not actively seeking and searching for men in my case (women for Stacey). One of the biggest casualties of this bizarre world we find ourselves in is that technology has created incredible amounts of connection between us and a bunch of people we do not know and really never will, but simultaneously this creates distance between real people and physical connections around us every day. My goal is now to never quit reaching for those further down "the road of life" from me.

Next, as I am journeying, learning, and progressing down my customized road of God's plan, while I am reaching to those further ahead, I find it incredibly life-giving to also be available to invest in and "pull" those who are younger than me. An interesting evolution has occurred in my mentoring development. As I continue to reach and find wise counselors to speak truth into my life, I find I have become more effective with those I might be mentoring. My natural tendency in these moments is to feel compelled to listen as a means to quickly process and offer up solutions based on my experience. However, this is not the approach I necessarily find most appealing about anyone who has ever mentored me. They poke and prod gently (sometimes not, if necessary) and pull out that which they already knew but knew would stick better if it came from my own realization. I have one mentor in particular who always asks, "Mike, what is God saying to you this morning?" Initially, I found this frustrating. "I don't know! I just want some answers to these problems I'm wrestling with." But in his investment, what I realized over time is he was pulling me up spiritually to where I needed to be. He did not say, "Hey, Mike, did you do your quiet time this morning? Have you been consistently praying about this issue?" This mentor knew from years of his own trials, wins, and a path that clearly reflected alignment with God's plan for his steps, that in asking me this simple question all of the other questions were implied. Now I can't say I have asked anyone I'm mentoring that exact question, but I have in recent years ended many conversations with, "Do you mind if I pray for you and what we've talked about?" I have never been turned down, and I am as encouraged and blessed in these moments as whomever I'm ending the conversation with.

Finally, there is perhaps no better opportunity to reach and pull than with our peers. These are the people in the trenches right there with us—those statistically we're most likely to live the most life with. They are figuring out a new marriage, stages of parenting, processing family dynamics, and all of the other life struggles and celebrations at the same time as us. They "get us" in unique ways others we're reaching and pulling with may not. However, because of pride and fear of not wanting to look bad, they can be the group we are least likely to deeply engage with. To be clear, in this confused world that works from very different plans and a completely warped grading scale, it is important to establish and maintain a safe place with our peers to help support and lift each other up. Here is the risk I know from my own life. If I do not manage this inner circle well—the one that equips us to be appropriately armed to go reach the world without getting crushed by it—and it becomes nothing more than a casual friend group chasing wealth, notoriety, or anything fleeting, then the likelihood that I am reaching or pulling with the two groups in the previous paragraphs is likely very low. And in that moment, it does not take very long at all to be operating almost solely on of my own plan.

This idea of reaching and pulling is a whole lot easier for me than it is to live out; but without God-fearing people in and around me with consistency, I lose the needed accountability that does not allow me to stray too far from the plan and path God is so excited to see me stay on. For this reason, I love this simple straightforward verse from I Thessalonians. In a world determined to dismantle and tear each other down, it is a simple truth bomb that our mission is to build each other up. I love that in supporting others in their quest to follow God's plan, it may be the single best activity that we can stay engaged with that in fact helps ensure we stay in alignment for our own path God has for us. Who are you reaching out to learn from, who are you helping pull up, and is your inner circle supporting God's plan for you?

20

TRAVEL LIGHT

IT IS ONE THING to pack for a family vacation, where it sometimes feels like we manage to squeeze the entire house into our SUV and the carrier on top. However, it is an entirely different exercise to pack for the purpose of going on a multiweek extreme adventure. For these trips, food and essentials must be calculated and measured (no Costco runs possible where these treks occur). While this likely will never be the kind of trip I will find myself on, I do enjoy living vicariously through others who are more inclined than me. It is remarkable how vital packing becomes, and what goes in on day one can have life or death implications on day thirty-three. Each ounce counts and only the most essential items can make the trip. On this lengthy journey through life, there is a difference between how I tend to travel on my own and how God desires me to move through life on His roadmap. I once heard the analogy of hiking with a backpack filled with large rocks. It does not take very long before the weight of the pack limits where you can go.

The first item we must be careful to manage and not allow to weigh us down are relationships. We have already established how vital key human connections impact our growth, maturity, and accountability. However, if I am not careful and strain these relationships, especially key ones, they can start to foster and harbor bitterness and unforgiveness. Left unchecked for very long, they inevitably become a hindrance to my ability to stay on course for God's plan for my life. In *Living Fearless*, Jamie Winship explores the idea of each of us fully living out our God-intended identity. Through his extensive experience working and living in some of the harshest conditions in the Middle East where hatred runs deep, he relays incredible personal stories where he describes forgiveness as the ultimate power play. On the surface, this sounds like some kind of negotiation tactic, but he articulates how incredibly powerful it is to love like Christ loves and extend this kind of love, manifested in the form of forgiveness. It defies our natural human laws of relational gravity, but it frees us to pursue God's plan for us unweighted by the burden of friction or tension.

Second, is the broad category of "stuff." We all realize that there is nothing on this earth we accumulate that will go with us when we die, but somehow it is always tempting to fall into the world's flow of collecting a wide range of things. There is nothing inherently wrong with any of it, but I am reminded Jesus's encounter with the young rich man recorded in the Gospels. He was ready to get on board with God's plan. He confidently rattles off a solid list of good things he is doing. Jesus, as only Jesus can, says, "Sounds great—sell everything you have, give it to the poor, and then you'll be ready." He already knew what would come next. This man, like all of us at some point, was hanging on to his wealth in a way that prevented him from being where God needed him. In recent years, I am even more focused on continuing to better manage my relationship to materialism, status, and other potential distracting things in my life that could be preventing God from doing everything He has planned. It is often easy to think God violently opposes these things, but He seems to simply want me to hold onto them loosely, never elevate their worth or importance above Him, and to ultimately find ways to utilize them within His Plan. When I do something amazing happens: the heaviness of that pressure to maintain and amass all these things starts to dissipate.

Finally, traveling lighter affords me the chance to always be ready for the twists and turns God's plan always seems to take. I think of David in the Old

God's Plan

Testament—a man given the incredible title of "a man after God's own heart." From shepherd boy to Goliath-slayer to Saul-escapee to King of Israel, his life and God-sponsored plan took all kinds of turns that required him to always be ready. The Psalms often depict someone deep in struggles and victories that come from His plan. But as David settles into being King over time (his office full of all the Philistine Super Bowl Trophies and King of the Year awards), he seems to be weighed down by all of that stuff. In some ways it feels like it detracted from his ability to finish strong and remain alert and ready for all that God wanted him to accomplish through Him. Somehow, as I round the corner to the back half of my life, while I want to be responsible and a good steward of my resources and provide for my family, I desire and continue to pray I would remain sensitive to the next season of my journey and excited about things that may fall outside of the "normal" progression the world is constantly messaging.

My human plan for my life relishes the perceived comfort of having a nice pile of earthly trinkets and accolades to grow, rely on, and utilize. God's plan requires me to let go of these things, not because He might not make them a part of my life, but so I can remain undistracted on my mission to go where He wants me to. Ironically, it is the things I expect to provide comfort that become burdensome "peace and joy" destroyers. It is when I really let go of these things to follow God more closely that I then feel relief and freedom that is impossible to recreate absent this step.

21

LOVING THE JONESES INSTEAD OF KEEPING UP WITH THEM

PERHAPS NOTHING IS MORE counterproductive to a life fully committed to adhering to the plan God has for us than worrying about devising a plan that simply mimics the lives of those we envy. The great irony is that we forgo the pursuit of something real and individualized and substitute that for chasing the biggest mirage there is. But this is hard—really hard—in today's social-media-driven culture where everything and anything available is flaunted in the most appealing ways possible. If I am not very careful and allow the pursuit of what I am seeing drive and help shape my plans, I am doomed to be anxious, empty, and certainly ineffective in carrying out God's plan for me.

First, I have found that when I pursue the status or possessions others have, it has extremely negative effects: losing sight of loving people. If anything, it is easy to start to dislike people. After all, in today's world, it will not take long to find someone who achieved success, and accumulated things, and become jaded and jealous. God's instructions for us while here on Earth are relatively simple (and simultaneously challenging) and involve loving Him with all of our heart and loving others as much as we love ourselves. There is no mention of us chasing others or what they have, and in fact, the tenth commandment instructs us to not envy what others have. Let's call that the "don't-try-to-keep-up-with-the-Joneses" commandment. Satan is clever—very clever. He loves for us to spend as much of, if not all, our lives in pursuit of this unattainable source of peace and joy through chasing what others have at the expense of never actually investing in people.

Second, the endless and fruitless pursuit of keeping up with what others are doing and buying not only drives my plan but will undoubtedly take me even further and quicker in a direction I will be less and less satisfied with. Without the single point of truth that God offers, I will flail from one rainbow-chasing effort to the next, with each leaving me more frustrated and less certain about who I am and what my purpose on Earth should be. On the other hand, while I continue to wrestle to get this right, what I can already say is that as I have doubled down my efforts to be "all-in" with God's plan, I have witnessed His unique way of opening and closing doors that I would not or could not. And even though He is unconventional in how He weaves experiences, opportunities, and people in and out of our lives, the Author of all life proves over and over to be a very capable "assembler of life plans."

Freedom. Now there is a word we all love to think and dream about, and depending on the context, it can mean different things. The kind of freedom that God offers through salvation and in "day-to-day" Christian living can be as good as it gets. I wish I operated out of this freedom 100 percent of the time, unfortunately, I do not. But as it relates to how I interact with and love on others, I find that when I am closely dialed into God and letting Him shape and inform this heavenly love, I then start to feel freedom from the worry about what others think or are doing. I get to enjoy freedom from all these unsavory and oppressive qualities that plague me when I am pursuing what others are doing or have. Out of this freedom, I can then love others and not look to my right or left to see what others are doing.

Who would have thought the Joneses could be so hard to keep up with and so distracting from the mission God put me on? What is often ironic is that many of the Joneses of today's world love the idea of someone else trying to keep up with them. Why? Because they are running as fast as they can toward their own Joneses and away from the emptiness that relentlessly chases them down. God would love nothing more than to pull you and me out of that race so that we can devote all of our energy and time to the pursuit of Him.

22

LOOKING BACK TO LOOK AHEAD

"But seek first his kingdom and his righteousness, and all these things will be given to you as well. Therefore do not worry about tomorrow, for tomorrow will worry about itself. Each day has enough trouble of its own."

Matthew 6:33-34

I AM A "POINT-A-TO-POINT-B" kind of a guy. I am black and white and type A, so I would like to think I do best with a clear mission and objective. I do like to have a couple of back-up plans and make every attempt to be discerning in terms of anticipating the unexpected. Uncertainty, or simply the lack of control, is unnerving and anxiety follows close behind. In contrast, a Christian life, lived out fully by entrusting God to direct my steps, is the complete opposite of what my human DNA craves and thinks it needs. I am never given much visibility of what might be next, but I am able to look back and see the intricate, interwoven details coming together. However, the type A in me, without this perfect roadmap, wants to know how close or far off I am on the path. The beauty of God's design seems to be that He chooses to leave much of the details mysterious this side of heaven. There will be unanswered questions and uncertainty that requires us to always stay humble and focus on listening to God's quiet whispers. I am learning, with much room left to grow, that in that look back, I can in fact see things that are indicators of things I need to change in order to get back on or stay on track with God's plan.

First, I find that the state of my relationships become very revealing in terms of whether I am leaning into my own strength and ideas or resting in what God wants for me. It always starts with where I am with my relationship with God. When I shortchange these moments, deficits in my other relationships soon follow. When I left my role in 2019, being honest about where my relationships with those closest to me were headed was one of the biggest reasons I knew God likely had a different direction for me to go in. In my own strength, I had run out of capacity to be all that Stacey and the girls needed me to be. I justified it for a while. After all, I was working like crazy to provide and protect them. The fact is all that work left me less and less physical time with my family and almost no emotional or mental gas left in the tank at all. I also discovered that I had fleeting amounts of time to just be available for others that needed my listening ear. Leaving the executive role and world was incredibly unnerving in many ways. He was not offering to reveal the roadmap ahead just yet. However, by recentering my relationship efforts, He validated that that difficult career decision I made was necessary in order to get me on the right track—His track.

Next lesson… as the adage goes, when you want to know where someone's priorities are, you need look no further than their checkbook. The world wants us to believe the treasure chest we accumulate is one of the best gauges of success here on Earth. God is not inherently opposed to these things, but humans are easily distracted and incapable of straddling the line between the things of this world and heavenly pursuits. When I pause to look back and start to see a pattern of more and more of time, energy and eventual stress fixated on the pursuit of possessions, I know I have drifted off course. What I appreciate about this passage in Matthew 6, and what I have continued to see in my own journey, is this: God has a way of gifting us with what we need when we need it. The caveat is we must stay close and depend on Him.

God's Plan

We all had fun with magnets as students. When putting two magnets together in one direction, it was impossible to keep them from coming together. However, turn one of them around and there was nothing that could bring the two ends together. Part of what made Jesus's time here on Earth so powerful is that He had this first magnetic effect on others; followers could not stay away from this life-giving and soul-searching engagements. Life hack alert: God's plan for all of us will involve this ingredient—it will include other people, and it should reflect and mirror the same magnetic effect that Jesus had. When I stray off course and become distracted with living out my plan, I become consumed. When I look back and start to see surmounting stress and angst, I repel people and isolate myself.

I have done a camp exercise with both of our daughters called the trust walk. They are blindfolded and I then give them four simple instructions: they can always trust me, they can ask me anything, they can only listen to my voice, and I will always be right by them. We then climb a hill, initially with me holding their hand and guiding them with my voice. At a set point, without alerting them, I let go of their hand and just use verbal commands. Finally, I am instructed not to say anything. Someone comes along and offers to help them. Eventually, if the exercise goes well, they remember the initial instructions and are able to get back on course to where they are supposed to go by asking me questions. This is a powerful exercise with endless points of application; but, perhaps most sobering and emotional for every dad I did this with is the powerful visual of how quickly we can all get distracted, forget the four basic instructions, and get off course. We may not love being blindfolded to exactly what is in front of us in life. But we always have access to His endless power and the reality that God is always right by us and knows where we need to go. With that truth, I can have a newfound confidence to press forward. I still remember walking back down the hill with Sophie and her commenting in surprise: "I climbed all of that?" She did, I can, and you can. We can be amazed at where we have been when we look back on God's plan in complete surrender.

23

CATCH AND RELEASE

BASED ON MY TRACK record, I am arguably least qualified to offer any analogy involving fishing so I will keep
this one high level so as not to risk completely exposing
my limited knowledge. There are certain places where
fishing is allowed, but where you should not count on
"your catch" feeding you for dinner because you must
immediately release your fish upon reeling it in. That
seems to contrast my plan against God's plan. Under
my plan, I tend to want to catch what life throws at
me and hold onto it. However, under God's plan, He
suggests, if not demands, that I immediately release it
to Him. This includes everything—what I am calling
the good, the bad, and the ugly.

We have all enjoyed mountain-top experiences: a
great family celebration, a promotion, acceptance into
a dream school, a financial windfall, etc. Under the
"my plan route," I am quick to assign credit to my

skill, personality, or hard work. The feeling of elation fades quickly and the need to recreate that feeling fuels the empty pursuit of the next mountain-top experience. Oh, I might be less brazen in my words or thoughts, but it is a slippery slope I have to fight off. In contrast, when I quickly celebrate these moments as God showing off and offer Him gratitude and praise, I release the moment and preserve the opportunity for God to continue to work freely in my life to create more moments which point others back to Him. When I take all the credit, others see me for better or often worse. But when I release that moment of goodness, they should quickly see a version of me that points them to Jesus.

The bad moments in life are likely the ones that, on the surface, most of us would claim we actually do want to quickly release to God. But if I am honest, as someone who wants to live under the illusion of having control more frequently than I would like, I often tend to try to solve the issue solo. I use the dial-a-friend option only after my attempts for resolution fail and I must call in God's reinforcements. The human condition craves smooth sailing, certainty, and comfort, yet God has designed us and this earthly existence to rotate around struggles where growth and a closeness to Him develop. It has been said that we are either going into a storm, are in the storm, or are coming out of the storm. When I acknowledge and embrace this reality and the idea that God's plan fully contemplates, if not demands these sharpening events, I am then freed to release these as they arrive. The older I get the more practical I find God, and I can almost hear Him saying in these moments: "Mike, I know this is hard. Talk to me about it. Release it to me. I know what's coming and how it weaves perfectly into what I have for you."

The ugly could be a variety of things, but as I think about them in my life, they are less circumstantial than they are the specific tendencies about us that have the potential to completely unravel us. For me, I think about impatience as just one example. It is problematic at times but can become ugly when I am tired or stressed and snap at those around me. At least in my life, these relatively small bursts, ugly and unnecessary, can create long-term wedges in key relationships. I must acknowledge these areas in my life and release them to God so that He can develop better patterns to help me stay on track with the larger plan He has built for me. I am not sure that any of these three can be ignored if I desire to be truly effective, but I find this area to be perhaps the most critical. If I fail to release these areas to God, I end up looking like a disjointed and inconsistent hot mess to anyone watching.

It can be frustrating to have to release a record-breaking fish right after going through the effort to reel

God's Plan

it in, but when it comes to life and all that it throws at us, there is perhaps nothing more life-giving than releasing everything to God and allowing Him to integrate each moment, gift, and tendency into His plan for each of us. Otherwise, we will be on a constant, exhausting, and losing quest to desperately hold on to and absorb each of these. Under this effort and plan, I might somehow survive, but I certainly will not thrive. Which route will you choose—surviving or thriving?

24

TAKE YOUR TIME AND HURRY UP

COMING OUT OF WEST Point, I had a plan for the next ten years and beyond. I hate to brag, but it was solid and practical. It was not particularly unique as I think several of us coming out of that environment had a similar one. In my largely uninformed twenty-two-year-old spiritual mind, I really thought I was freeing God up to help other, more confused, people with their plans since I knew there would be parts of mine that required His assistance. The plan was this: I would serve my five-year commitment to the Army, get out of the military, go back to a top business school, get settled into a job and get to some safe, yet-to-be-defined place of financial security, before marrying someone a little younger and starting a family. But as usual, God was way ahead of me. As logical as my plan might have been, it was not His best for me. I encountered some relational challenges, doubled down on my commitment to trusting God, then met and married Stacey, who is a little older than me (to be clear beautiful, ageless, and the youngest person at heart I have ever met) while I was still in the Army. I did go to business school, and we started a family as soon as we moved back to Texas. I look back now and continue to be amazed about the perfection of His plan, but more importantly, I really hate to think about the complete fallacy of thinking mine was better.

I have learned something about the nature and character of God through this experience and even more so in the last few years. God is incredibly patient. After all, He is the just-in-time God who is never early or late. However, His patience and my stubbornness are costly in terms of living out His ideal plan. Time here on Earth is a vicious and ruthless reality that stops for no one and is evenly distributed to all of us in the same quantities each day. The more of it I devote to the pursuit of a plan based my own limited capabilities, the less of it is left to devote to what He intended. He will always be there to step in whenever I allow Him, but His desire is for me, and each of us, to reach a place of total surrender sooner than later. I do not know that my human brain will ever be able to completely comprehend the notion that the Creator of the universe sincerely and passionately desires me to invite Him into my life so He can have the opportunity to do things in and through me that are far beyond what I am otherwise capable of.

As I have checked off more and more milestones in life that once seemed liked distant moments in the future, it is apparent that I must continue to develop an active dialog with God through prayer. When He speaks, I need to be able to recognize His voice and act on it. Otherwise, I risk losing valuable time wondering and guessing what I am hearing and making decisions without a clear sense of whose plan they are actually a part of. With each season of life, the brevity and frailty of life become more and more apparent. Today is all you and I are promised.

Godly balance seems to be the Jesus way. You can feel a cadence in His life on Earth that was busy but intensely purposeful, yet also included quiet and rest. A feverish pace seems doomed to end in complete exhaustion, no matter how great the seeming cause or purpose. A life of endless rest results in missing our purpose and ignoring our life mission. But when I am intentionally seeking balance where recharging involves not just mindless nothing but quieter moments to hear and understand what God has next and activity is purposeful people centric, then I am more than likely making real progress in the direction of the plan God wants me on.

25

KINGLY LESSONS

KING SAUL, DAVID, AND Solomon are well documented central figures of the Old Testament. We are gifted with riveting detail of their thoughts, actions, successes, conquests, and more. At least in the case of David and Solomon, we even have their own books in the Bible where their own God-breathed words and prayers are recorded and often recited. We have a really strong sense of where these men stood and how they performed in terms of the plan they followed. David and Solomon, while far from perfect, have lives that reflect God's fingerprints. Saul, however, stumbled frustratingly through a life full of promise but ultimately marred and undone by a reluctance to relinquish full control to God. For most other Kings of Israel noted in the Old Testament, there is often only one of two phrases that accompany their mile marker in the Bible: "He did what was right in the eyes of the Lord" or "He did what was evil in the eyes of the Lord." This is a scary thought. What if my life can only be captured at the end by a couple of very distinct and different phrases that essentially reflect my willingness and ability to follow my plan versus God's? In these kings, I see a couple of pieces of compelling evidence that make me want to fall in line with God's plan.

First, even in these short and abbreviated descriptions, I commonly see the people (or in this case, the kingdom) around these kings benefit or suffer from their approach and their plan. Chaos, suffering, and turmoil are common outcomes from kings who wandered off on their life plan adventure. But none of us has to be a king to drag other people into our decisions and approaches to life. Hopefully, it is completely unappealing to create self-imposed problems in my own life. It should take me to an entirely new level of reflection to consider the implications and ripple effect of my life on those around me of the plan I follow. But there is no reason for this to be negative. There is equally available and compelling evidence that those in and around the king who are honoring and following God also enjoyed the benefits and joy of this approach. I see it in my own life with my family. When I am pushing and grinding through my own power, the tenseness and pressure I feel does not take long to leak out and create tension inside of my family.

My flawed plan leaves me emotionally breathless and feeling out of sorts and incapable of leading, loving, and caring for my family as God intended. Conversely, when I lean into where God is wanting to take me, His peace and calmness operates above and outside of circumstances and breathes life into Stacey and our two girls. There is a powerful effect of having our family operating in unison, with each member operating out of their God-sponsored plan but in harmony with everyone else's.

Next, I find a generational and legacy component to these notes about each of these kings that is constructive. In its simplest form, it is easier to follow God's plan if following it has been modeled for you. As the saying goes, most of what our children learn is caught and not taught. The most meaningful gift I can offer to our two daughters is not a trust fund but a faith legacy that involves not just the most critical decision to accept Christ, but also the subsequent commitment to really seek and desire to follow His plan. I love that in the not-so-uncomplicated handoff between King David, amazingly known as the man after God's own heart, and his son, Solomon, God grants Solomon a wish for anything. He humbly asks for wisdom and discernment. While not all that David modeled for Solomon was positive, I am left to believe that Solomon observed enough in David's life to want to launch his role as king where David left off.

But in these "king" snippets I see encouragement for those without this legacy. It is an opportunity and challenge to reset and change things. One of the best examples is King Josiah. To say the spiritual example cards were stacked against him is an understatement. His dad and grandfather were both described as wicked, and he only became king after his dad was assassinated when he was only eight years old. But Josiah, under God's plan, reversed course completely and reset his family lineage. The account recorded in 2 Kings is almost gushing as it describes him by saying, "And he did what was right in the eyes of the Lord and walked in all the ways of David his father, and he did not turn aside to the right or to the left." In a world today filled with new levels of brokenness, we still serve the God of fresh starts and new beginnings. There is this unique blended challenge for each of us to leverage the entire spiritual legacy while being solely accountable and responsible for the decisions and actions we take moving forward to honor God's plan.

Each word contained in the Bible is God-breathed, but it is still easy for me to blow right past some of these king names and footnotes. However, when I pause to recognize that each of these represent decisions, lives, and potential (met and unmet), it becomes a place from which I am convicted and inspired to not miss the opportunities in front of me. I desire to be the kind of man that "did what was right in the eyes of the Lord." How will you be described?

26

SUPER MODEL

"...not my will, but yours be done."

Luke 22:42

NEVER BEFORE AND NEVER since has God's plan for someone's life been as flawlessly executed as it was for the thirty-three years Jesus lived on this earth. And there has been no bigger purpose for someone's life than the incredible, mankind-saving mission Jesus was on to bring eternal life to all of mankind. Beyond that most important treasure, all of us were also gifted with the incredible and faithful model of the plan-following that He lived while here on Earth. He arguably had access to one of the most incredible arsenals of self-centered plans. He could have had the latest model of chariot, the most exotic palace, and ultimately made Soloman's worldly excessiveness look mediocre. But He did the exact opposite in His unwavering quest to do exactly what God sent Him to

God's Plan

Earth for. Beyond the countless, patient parables and direct lessons Jesus left, the life He lived and attitude He had is a remarkable model for all of us to follow. Three of the many things that I see in Him are what I am calling the three Ps.

First, Jesus was in a constant posture of prayer. He never walked into situations without giving them up to God in prayer. It would be easy to assume that Jesus and the Father had a quick pow-wow before Jesus left Heaven and pre-determined His role, tasks, mission, and ability, and that was that. However, Jesus very explicitly and intentionally models for us the closeness He had with God, and the closeness we also must have to operate in constant alignment with Him. Jesus was always very intentional about His prayer life. He dedicated time and place for very specific times with God, and I see this consistency and resulting impact come through by constant connection to the Father who sent Him.

Second, in Jesus I see incredible thoughtfulness in the places He put Himself in to create opportunities to maximize His impact. His mission on Earth was to model for us how to live, how to love, and, ultimately, how to draw others to a saving relationship with Him. When I think about the recorded accounts in which Jesus constantly put Himself and why, I see a brilliant and flawless example for how I should and constantly seek the places and situations that maximize my God-sponsored life plans. Even as a young boy, we find Jesus "lost" from His earthly parents. Where do they finally find Him? In the temple "doing His father's work." One of the things that I am observing and noticing is, recently, the world's plan for life often centers around a goal of ultimately finding our way into this supposed zen-like physical and emotional place. It is a place where routine is calm and relaxing (coffee, golf, walks, cool breeze, etc.) and problems are hedged against. I do not think God is against thoughtful planning as we go through life, but I am more and more confident that it is not God's intent for my life to strive toward a place that takes me completely out of the flow of where His work needs to happen.

Finally, and perhaps most obvious and apparent, is the intense care and love for people that Jesus constantly demonstrates. The tension between truth and love that He perfectly balanced made Him an even more riveting and compelling figure to not only listen to, but also give up everything to follow. He never compromised the message but was freewheeling with His interactions and the people He engaged with. Even with His dying breaths on the cross, He was concerned about the criminal next to Him and making sure His mother was taken care of. It is remarkable on so many levels and it defies nearly everything in that moment that anyone can imagine. But it was this careful and sincere attention that He gave to His mission of saving all people that has ultimately provided the simple but life-saving roadmap that Christians can follow. One of the quickest ways I know I have gotten off path is when my love and care for people wavers—when people and all of their idiosyncrasies start to repel me. I cannot even imagine how hard it must have been at times for Jesus to see and feel all these terrible human tendencies yet still feel sincere concern and care for all. If Jesus, in spite of all of these things, could not be deterred in loving others, it should encourage all of us to pursue the same.

None of us should be frustrated or discouraged in pursuing a flawless role model in Jesus. This is the model we all need and should want. An imperfect God would not be worth following. What I really hope we find comforting and reassuring is just seeing what this perfect alignment with God's plan can and should look like. God wants us to study and mimic the life Jesus led, period.

27

ONE DEGREE OFF

EVERY CHRISTIAN CAN CLAIM a story of a 180-degree turn from an eternity apart from Christ to one forever in His presence. No one in the Bible experienced this complete reversal more dramatically than Paul (the Christ follower formerly known as Saul). He went from one of the biggest nemeses of the early Christian movement to the main author of the New Testament and the main early messenger of the Gospel to non-Jewish people. It is one of the few times we see God insert Himself directly into someone's life and almost demand a complete 180. However, it is perhaps more telling and powerful to read these letters from Paul after this turnaround and witness the ongoing tension and effort he made to stay on course with God's plan. While none of us will be able to live perfectly, we must develop a sensitivity and humility to recognize when we are even one degree off God's course for us. When

I go too long on that path and am off just a degree, I end up much further away from the destination than I wanted and what God wants. It is always much more difficult to course correct from being one degree off than it is to quietly drift off course. There are three "As" that have been useful in my far-from-perfect quest to avoid getting off course.

First, I am reminded here that God is an "any-time-anywhere" mover in our lives. He is always ready for me and all of us to fall into alignment with His will and plan. It is not my timeline and perceived understanding of the facts around my life that determine and/or inform God how and when to begin His work. It is easy for me to project onto God, even through prayer sometimes, how and when I would ideally prefer for Him to divulge and execute His upgraded plan. But as life happens more and more, I am reminded that He does not and will not operate like that. If I want to avoid the drifting away from God's plan, then I need to be constantly asking Him to reveal His plan and fall into alignment with that.

Second, God is kind to put other people around us who love us; the plan God has for us is second to none and He knows we need accountability to stay on His path. God has used people in powerful ways throughout my life to offer up prayer, support, and accountability. These people know about the desire I have to walk closely with Him, and they speak love and truth into me from this perspective. I know I am in a bad place when I find myself isolating and not wanting to engage with anyone. In that place of isolation, I am far more vulnerable, if not destined, to drift off course; but when I am vulnerable and have already established a tribe of trusted people in my inner circle, I can see and hear exactly what I need to get back into a place where God can freely work His plan for my life again.

Finally, to stay the course and avoid drifting, I must recognize that God is always available. I have had seasons (and we all do) when I felt very distant from God. In my mind, I did not see enough evidence of His working in my life. I am always reminded of the oldie but goodie poems out there, like "Footprints in the Sand". The author starts by bemoaning the fact that in these certain seasons of life two pairs of footprints in the sand became one pair. They assume that means that those were tough moments when God abandoned them. But the author is quietly assured that those times were in fact moments when God was carrying them. It is a lot more fun to read this poem than to live its reality in our own lives. When I can embrace and take great comfort in knowing there will never be a gap in my life where God is unaccounted for, then there should never be a reason for me to try to take matters into my own hands and risk getting off course.

Once thrown to the ground and blinded by God, Paul set off on a journey according to God's plan that was nothing short of extraordinary. Paul was keenly aware of his own shortcomings and the need to keep his unwavering focus on his new life mission. One thing I appreciate about Paul was his use of sports analogies. Often, these centered around running the race of life that God predetermined for each of us. It is impossible to successfully complete our race without constantly checking and adjusting the path we are on. Being dependent on God for direction does not make us weak, but rather, in God's perfect economy, makes us incredibly strong and confident in the faith we have and path we are on.

28

THE ANSWER IS YES

"Trust in the Lord with all your heart and lean not on your own understanding; in all your ways submit to him, and he will make your paths straight."

Proverbs 3:5-6

I REMEMBER THE FIRST time that I interacted with a friend, and I started to ask a question that had the sound of a potential favor. But before I could get my request out, I was quickly greeted with the response, "The answer is yes. What is the question?" I have subsequently used this approach with someone else and heard the story of this response a few other times. It is bold and demonstrates a level of relationship that has a depth capable of hearing any request and already being completely at ease with a positive response. I want that in my relationship with God—to be so utterly in tune with Him that I need not hear His thoughts for His next plans for me to be able to answer "yes." When I think about the human connections I have that allow this exchange to happen, I think about a couple of needed elements for this to work consistently in my life.

I heard church-planting Pastor Boto Joseph say that we cannot love someone we do not know. It sounds so simple, but this hits me right between the eyes. In the couple of instances I can think of, we had history with each other. We had invested in getting to know each other to the point where we fully trusted each other's motives, alignment around outcomes, and shared desires for the best for the other. I fear that where I have drifted off course in my life spiritually, it is because of my lack of pursuit of God through prayer, quiet times, and a sincere desire to know Him better. Pastor Joseph also pointed out a remarkable distinction between Christianity and the other major religions. Rather than us being in a constant and fruitless pursuit of a higher, unreachable power, we in fact serve a God who has and will always be in pursuit of us. I do not have to guess about the plan He has in mind for me so long as I am also in pursuit of Him. We then have the opportunity to come together, and I can always launch with "yes" before fully understanding the question.

The Answer Is Yes

Next, I need to be spiritually opportunistic and predetermine answers to God as He directs my steps. When I called this friend, they had already determined that "yes" answer before I ever uttered a word. They had created the emotional, mental, physical space and capacity to handle whatever question and resulting task I might throw at them. It is a given that God will in fact always be ready for whatever I throw at Him. However, I, unfortunately, am anything but a given. The disciplines and tools that allow me to know and love God better also have the effect of giving me more confidence to lean fully into these moments of great uncertainty and say "yes... now what's the question?" There is a place I am prone to slide into where I pick and choose when I respond this way—where I am selective instead of opportunistic and where I say, "Before I say 'yes' can you let me know what you're thinking, how hard it's going to be, and how soon a good outcome, as defined by me, will be."

Finally, this sort of "yes-first-question-later" approach is the ultimate trust-fall. It is the place where I have given over full creative and operational control of my life to God. I have made a decision to embrace and celebrate whatever God might ask of me no matter how crazy it sounds. Proverbs 3:5-6, for this reason, will always be my rallying cry and life verse. It contains words I do not naturally love when it describes my

131

God's Plan

role—words like: "all of your heart," "lean not on your own understanding," and "submit to Him." But it ends with words I find incredibly reassuring: "He will make your paths straight." The answer to Him always must be "yes" because His desire for me and His plan is nothing but the most fulfilling, God-honoring life.

There will likely be very few people in any of our lives that allow us to start with a definitive answer before hearing the request or question. But God is the one constant in our Christian existence that invites us into this exact "yes-first" back-and-forth for the duration of our lives here on Earth. The uncertainty and lack of control can be difficult for me to accept, but when I am in constant communication with Him, I learn to not only accept but crave this interaction. Philippians 1:6 anticipates and encourages us to seek this life of Christ-sponsored adventure by letting us know what God starts He finishes. His plan for us is not only the best one, but one that, when we say "yes" over and over, IS the plan God is 100 percent committed to seeing through to completion.

29

EXPECT A FIGHT – STAY IN THE FIGHT

"Be alert and of sober mind. Your enemy the devil prowls around like a roaring lion looking for someone to devour."

I Peter 5:8

AS CHRISTIANS, WE SERVE an active God who is always moving in us, working in us, and pursuing us. This is great news because we are also pitted against an extremely active enemy who is committed to our demise. He knows our eternity is secure but that does not mean he can't and won't work overtime to make us ineffective in our ability to point others to the same end point. While God's plan for each of us is custom in nature, we are all following the same Great Commission. I have discovered a correlation that is as strong and predictable as death and taxes. When my heart and mind connect in pursuit of God's plan and start to gain traction, like clockwork, I can expect Satan to go into overdrive. In the struggle, we learn. In the learning, we grow our faith. In our growth, we mature and in maturity, we reach others. If Satan can be relentless enough to get us to give up before we start reaching others, in a sense, he wins. Just putting this on paper makes me nervous, because I am writing what I need to hear early and often in my own life. Staying engaged in that fight that is ultimately latching onto the plan God has penned for my time on Earth requires many things, but I will focus on the three Cs.

The first is communication. I John 4:4 states the obvious, likely because I am in constant need of being reminded of the obvious: The God I have inside of me as a Christian is greater than the enemy that lurks in every corner of this world. As such, it becomes critical that I am in constant communication with Him. While not as consistent as I would like, over the last several years, I have become a fan of keeping a prayer journal. There are many unexpected blessings that come through the discipline of writing out my prayer life, and I am constantly looking for ways to deepen this. Journaling forces me to be more intentional with documenting my running dialog with God. It allows me to mature in faith as my prayers shift from things that matter to me to things that matter to God. And perhaps biggest of all, in recording prayers and needs, it becomes an incredible historical record of answered prayers and God's consistency. I have sometimes worried that during a dry season my prayers read like some of those cries from the Psalms. While I do not think God expects or wants us to remain in these places forever, I am convinced He wants me to constantly be grappling and fighting to stay connected to Him, ask tough questions, expect big answers, and keep an always deepening relationship with Him.

Second, we must stay connected with others. Some of this closely ties to the first of prayer. I look at big milestones and places in my life, and it is impossible to not think of several key people in my life at that moment who I know for certain committed to praying on my behalf. This is big. Isolation is one of the biggest tools in Satan's toolbox and he is using it with incredible effectiveness in today's world. We were built to love, support, and lift up our fellow man. While God's plan for my life might be specific and unique to me, there is not a chance that I can find my way to success without constant and complex interconnection to others, who are hopefully also following God's same direction for their lives. It is powerful when I start to recognize and actively engage others, praying into their lives and God-plans at the same time they are committed to prayerfully supporting mine.

God's Plan

Finally, we need a stubborn conviction in our pursuit of God and what He wants for and from us. Even in preparing to write this second book, about two to three weeks after committing to finishing it, I just felt that there was an unusual number of things working against this big effort. I was frustrated because Stacey and I had prayerfully arrived at the decision for me to do this despite it being during a busy season for our family. I had to chuckle in some way because what I came to realize is that the very essence of committing to putting these thoughts on paper to encourage others to stretch and pull toward God's intended best for their lives is in absolute conflict with the roaring lion that wants to devour you and me. I reached out to a couple of prayer warriors and asked for their faithful prayers during this writing effort. It has been far from easy, and I still feel the enemy of self-doubt, fear of failure, and other unproductive thoughts, but I am much more encouraged.

It is easy to look at the Old Testament and see all the battles, wars, and conflicts and compare it to a modern-day Christianity that sometimes fixates on the more loving parts of Jesus in the New Testament. While the God of the universe has elevated the idea of love beyond anything we could comprehend, I really appreciate the idea that God is an absolute powerhouse who demands respect, is the ultimate GOAT, and is in my corner asking me to do hard things against some tough odds yet is committed to being there every step of the way. He is not a distant order-taker who's handed me a map and said, "Good luck!" God is armed and ready to help me take the fight to the enemy. It will look different for all of us, but it will most likely also look very different than the twenty-five-year-younger version of us was thinking it would be. That's okay—it's actually great. Let's roll!

30

TURN-BY-TURN NAVIGATION

WITH A COUPLE OF relatively new and budding drivers at our house, there are a few opinions on the best way to use modern navigation technology to get from point A to point B. Everyone else but me seems to appreciate the turn-by-turn navigation that even adds a voice to accompany the visual cues on the screen. It gives you just enough information and directions to get you to the next point. On the other hand, I prefer to punch in the address and I want to see the entire route. I want to know where I'm going and be able to zoom in for detail, if needed. I could attempt to convince everyone reading this that I have cornered the market on the best way to navigate in the car, but I suspect that I would likely enjoy the same success rate that I have convincing those at my house. Unfortunately, what I am successfully doing with navigating in my driving life does not translate well in my pursuit of God's plan.

God's Plan

What drives me crazy when I ride with someone else in my family as they use the turn-by-turn feature is actually what calms everyone else. The fact that the map is giving them just enough to make the next turn allows them not to worry about things they can't see yet. The truth is the navigation system is calculating, accounting for traffic and other factors, and allowing the driver to simply focus on the here and now. I have a hard time with this both on the road and in life, and I feel somewhat at ease sharing this because my experience suggests that I am in good company. I disguise it as wanting to help, be proactive, and stay a few steps ahead. But what typically happens in life is that I invite a level of anxiety and fear about the future that I am simply incapable of processing and digesting. I love the way Matthew 6:34 puts it: Don't sweat tomorrow—it's got enough problems of its own and can worry about itself.

I admire the confidence my family has in this tool. My wife always very calmly and correctly points out after we have navigated our way somewhere using turn-by-turn: "See. We got here." And she is right, and I have nothing to show for any questioning I might have had. God wants the same level of trust from you and me for where He wants to take us. "Hey wait, God, I think I know this part of town… we should avoid it…. Wait, God, I think we took a wrong turn." And

Turn-by-Turn Navigation

while it feels very disconcerting to not know exactly what the destination He has punched in is, given that I have secured my eternity in Him, shouldn't I be incredibly confident and comfortable in the earthly journey He prescribes?

One of the funnier moments, although not necessarily that way at the time, happens when we miss a directed turn. The navigation system quickly gets to work, working its algorithmic magic to reroute us in a way that still allows us to arrive where we intended. But it is not ideal and often costs us time. God is the Master Reroute Artist, which is incredibly reassuring given that outside of Jesus, no one I am aware of in history has not had multiple reroutes in life. We are imperfect and make rash and even poor decisions that have consequences. Yet, when it comes to the big directional trajectory of our lives, when given big directions where God is pointing us to go left and our human nature is telling us to go right, I am at a place where I want to fight the urge to go right and embrace the uncertainty and lean into what God has in store. It becomes easier as I become more comfortable with God's limitless love and become completely confident that He has ways of weaving uncertain and uncomfortable moments today into amazing milestones tomorrow.

I remain unconvinced that the way I navigate in the car is incorrect, but I am absolutely certain that using this approach to fall into line with God's plan is a recipe for disaster. I have taken increasing comfort in recent years with the idea that God, I believe, wants us to continue improving and learning all the way up until our last breath here on Earth. There is no cruise control that He offers in the last third of our life, no such notion of spiritual retirement, and no plateau. He intends to keep us on our toes in this turn-by-turn life that He carefully crafted. Buckle up!

31

CONTENTMENT IN THE JOURNEY

"I have learned the secret of being content in any and every situation, whether well fed or hungry, whether living in plenty or in want. I can do all this through him who gives me strength."
Philippians 4:12-13

HUMANS ARE RESTLESS CREATURES. My plans, at their best and worst, are constant feats of striving and reaching in the hopes that I might somehow reach an elusive plateau of accomplishment or recognition or wealth that leaves me satisfied. These feelings are based on human metrics that are a constantly moving target. Discontentment is the best way to describe this hamster wheel of highs and lows we will face without question under the power of our own plans. Conversely, contentment might be the single biggest draw for me following God's plan. When I put a visual to this word, I can picture a place I love by a stream or calm lake in Colorado on a perfect summer day. But unlike my plan, as this verse from Philippians challenges and charges me, it is more than a feeling and has no correlation to worldly based metrics. It is all made possible because all of the power I will ever need resides right here inside of me through Jesus. So, what does this look like and not look like in my life?

Anxiety, worry, and fear might be the biggest epidemics the world faces in today's volatile environment. Despite the world's denial of a God, in His absence and left to our own power, we still somehow all come prewired with a nagging truth bomb inside of us that recognizes this: our own abilities are extremely limited and these paralyzing attributes (anxiety, worry, fear) are inevitable byproducts of our own efforts to reach and grab what the world without God offers. But there is a reason that "fear not" appears so many times in the Bible. Fear turns out to be a common, albeit no less devastating, part of human existence on Earth. At least in my life, it seems impossible for any of these traits to persist when I am content and in alignment with God's plan.

Next, I do not find that I just pray one morning and slide into this immediate and peaceful state of contentment. We are all wired differently and will likely have to ask God to grow us into His desired state of contentment. My experience is that this takes a lot of heart work, which is hard work as Pastor Gregg Matte frequently says. I am an achiever with a black-and-white, realistic bend that borders on pessimistic. I naturally want to mitigate risk, have several back-up plans, and be ready for anything. But this can breed all of the unsavory feelings above and leave me hanging onto issues longer than God ever intended me to. God wants our surrender and the complete peace that follows, knowing that He is working and weaving each of these circumstances into His plan for us. I do not believe God ever expects or wants passiveness out of any of us. But our striving should shift from an exhausting self-push to a real-time walk with God in every part of our lives.

Gratitude is the secret sauce in contentment. When earthly outcomes no longer matter the way they used to and my focus shifts to a constant recognition of His perfect work in my life, then I can claim what Paul does in this powerful verse. I continue to work toward this place of peace and joy. One of the more advanced and difficult areas of growth I have encountered is the way God answers prayers. When I pray for more patience (and I do), His gift of more patience comes in the form of new situations that require patience. At least for me, the better I do in one area, the greater the tests He puts in front me. It pushes and pulls me

God's Plan

spiritually, but it ultimately is the only way I can experience improvements. So, when I pray for contentment (and I do) and the backend byproducts of peace and joy, I find that God, in fact, puts me in situations that are not easy to be content in without complete reliance on Him.

I remember talking to an entrepreneurial friend who was further down a path I was considering diving down. I was battling fears of the unknown. I do not even know if my friend is a Christian, but he shared that part of what made him successful as an entrepreneur. He did not fear going to zero. He simply meant that whatever new venture he took on, he was thoughtful but ultimately tried to never allow the fear of going financially broke prevent him from making a good investment decision. God has something far better to offer you and me when it comes to contentment, peace, and joy. When we lean into the plan God has, we may or may not end up at zero, however the world defines that, but we can be at total peace that we are exactly where God intended. We know that if God is for us (and He is), who can be against us?

32

PILES ON THE SIDE OF THE ROAD

"Do not store up for yourselves treasures on earth, where moths and vermin destroy, and where thieves break in and steal. But store up for yourselves treasures in heaven, where moths and vermin do not destroy, and where thieves do not break in and steal. For where your treasure is, there your heart will be also."

Matthew 6:19-21

WE HAVE LIVED IN Houston long enough now to have experienced a few major weather events. There are a couple of unforgettable images that jump to mind in the aftermath of these storms, especially flood related. First are the more traumatic drives through an affected neighborhood a week or two later. There are piles of almost everything from inside the house now in a soaked on the curb. It is almost like someone's entire life and history is captured in one place that will eventually be scooped up, taken away, and never seen again. The next image is the one in these same neighborhoods of family, friends, and neighbors rallying around each other to clean up and start to restore and repair the damage done. There is a focused common effort and people from all walks of life rebuild together. I cannot help but think that God wants me and all of us to be reminded of these two images when it comes to our life plan. When I do not routinely inventory my plan with Him and it becomes more mine than God's, then I am accumulating things that are doomed to be part of a heaping pile of "really didn't matter" at the end of my life. But, when I press into God's plan, driven by relational efforts, I am gifted with a wide range of eternal and lasting engagements and connections with Him and others that can never be forgotten.

Here are a couple of things I have observed about the piles in my life. First, they sneak up on me. There is nothing inherently bad about having anything in our homes (and lives). We need some of these just to exist in the world we live in. But the frequent comment from anyone that owns a home for any length of time sounds something like, "How did I get this much stuff?" It just becomes a more jarring observation when it quickly becomes consolidated in a pile in your front yard. It is easy for me similarly to build my life around a quickly growing collection of things that will not ultimately matter. Perhaps more problematic for me is the opportunity costs of these piles. The time, effort, and resources that each required means that other things and people God had for me in His plan simply never made it into my life.

There is a better path forward for all of us. God's plan uses these piles to develop relationships that matter and last. God never has an expiration on His plan and wants us to jump all the way in. I remember when Stacey and I were contemplating a home purchase and praying through this decision. We needed more space but neither of us wanted to make the house about us. We prayed that if God wanted us to have the home, that we would give it away as a place where people connected, where it felt like a safe place and one that honored God. It has been powerful to see God answer this prayer and allow us to use our home to serve. When I am prone to get caught up in some of the inevitable stress and drama that comes through home ownership, Stacey is always good to bring me back to the place we started. When I am able to give up my tendencies, God is able to do far more work in and through me. He can do it through you, too.

Selfishly, I would be just fine if somehow Houston stopped being the recipient of these occasional stressed-filled moments—probably in a similar way that I wish

God's Plan

life would lose the unwanted parts. But God's plan seems to be at its best when I am working with Him through all the ups and downs. He wants to show off and let all of us see just how capable He is. When I get distracted on this "pile-collection quest" in my own power, I rob Him of the chance to do this work, and I rob those around me of the opportunity to see His work being done through me.

33

FAMILY PLANNING

"Start children off on the way they should go, and even when they are old they will not turn from it."
Proverbs 22:6

THE GREATEST THING THAT Stacey and I can pass along to our two daughters before they leave our home, next to introducing them to a personal relationship with Jesus, is to model a faith walk that follows God's plan. Going to church regularly, church camps, and all the Christian activities are great, but if the adage that "most of what we learn is caught and not taught" is correct, then we must be on a lifelong quest to be authentically living out the words we listen to and sing on Sundays. Afterall, it is this same level of prayerful intentionality of the two generations ahead of me that has led me here today. However, there are a few potential obstacles that will limit my effectiveness in transferring this legacy of Christ-centered plan-following.

First, we cannot be passive. Especially for men and husbands, it can be tempting to check out where it matters the most: at home. I can justify this poor behavior without too much effort. Work is intense and is needed to provide for the good of the family. Stacey is a natural nurturer and does an excellent job working with and developing our daughters. I do not often know how to be emotionally and spiritually vulnerable while offering security and leadership. Here is the ugly reality of where we find ourselves today when I reread this verse from Proverbs. We instill these values and invest deeply in our girls, so they have deep, strong roots when they leave home. We want them firm in their foundation so they can survive the barrage of non-Christian views they will immediately be confronted with. I cannot afford to be passive. If I expect them to be prepared to handle this environment, I cannot deflect and defer my roles onto Stacey or anyone else. I must remain invested and trust God to work His plan for my life, even if it includes shifting away from areas like work.

Second, there is no substitute for time, which, when it comes to children and family, is another spelling for l-o-v-e. When you are grinding hard, it is easy to try to bracket and build time boxes. These can be carefully planned family trips where we try to unplug and be more present and that is necessary and

Family Planning

often life-giving. However, as someone who was a slow learner in this area when the girls were younger, I discovered it is the consistent small investments of time over an extended period that really established relationship and earned the trust necessary for our children to take hold of our faith as their own. It is the nightly conversations we had around the dinner table and during bedtime routines that they remember. It is the seemingly ordinary yet necessary ride home from school or practice where real conversations happened. If I do not predetermine to make myself available and make these happen, they simply will not. I remember going to a father-daughter camp with our teenage daughters. It was an incredible time and every father-daughter combination there was heavily invested in their relationship. We all wanted to get to a deeper place in our relationships. But it was hard to see some of the pairs struggling to connect because the investment of time had never been there. Now presented with a solid week together, the dad was confronted with the reality of the difficult, albeit never impossible with God, task of playing catch up.

Finally, we must understand the nature of the true relationship we have with our children. They are ultimately God's children. He was kind and gracious enough to give them to us and help us nurture and raise them before we send them off into the world. This is

God's Plan

really hard for us parents to acknowledge, accept, and embrace. We invest so much into these children, and it is easy to want to hold on so tightly and control everything we can. But just like everything else with our God-sponsored plan, the goal is to lean into Him and give up our children. If we do not, their successes and failures will start to be become a pride-fueled roller-coaster. And if we ultimately desire is for them to leave our home excited and confident in God's plan, then we are simply the vessels selected to help Him create this passion and desire.

Parenting is the most challenging, humbling, invigorating, and exhausting endeavor Stacey and I have tackled. I can easily come up with shortcomings I have (and I do need to be incredibly self-reflective and honest), but I have found that when my vertical relationship with God is in a good place, then my relationship with Stacey gets into a good place, and from there our ability to be effective parents grows exponentially.

We should be ferocious in our pursuit to love people on all corners of the earth. However, as our daughters have gone through various stages of life, I have been challenged and reminded that the most obvious and important people we can and should positively impact are the ones we see every day. As our teenage daughters have begun to shift into this next phase of life and started to really own their faith, it has been incredible to watch. I have a very long list of things I wish I had done differently, but God in His mercy seems to do a great job of filling in the gaps I am prone to leave everywhere. So many of Jesus's parables involved strong family imagery. Christianity is the ultimate family affair and heritage a key part. But what I love about God's approach to this is that it is never fear based. It is anchored in each of us simply living life in a such a profound Christ-centric way that our children and those around us have a difficult time imagining living any other way. Why would they?

34

CLICKS AND STICKS

WE ALL READ A book like this hoping and praying that there is something between the front and back covers that clicks and sticks with us in a lasting and meaningful way. I was reminded of this after writing my first book, *The Legacy Business*, as people kindly sent me notes of encouragement to let me know what specific chapter and idea was impactful to them and their specific season or challenge in life. These nuggets ran the gamut and reminded me that each of us comes into these moments from our own unique places, and that God uses different pieces to connect with us where we are. It is my prayer that there has been something I have attempted to convey that connects with you about the critical nature and importance I am seeing with increasing intensity in my own life for the need to be completely sold out to the plan God has for each of us.

God's Plan

For me, there seems to be two necessary ingredients for impact to be fully maximized. First, and potentially overly apparent, is that something must click with me. It is an "ah-hah" moment when a verse or a point hits me in a way I never thought of before, and it immediately connects to something I have or am experiencing in my life. It is the thought that rolls around in my head for several days after I read or hear it. It might even require some internal processing or wrestling, but it suddenly helps explain something I've been living or dealing with.

Secondly, whatever clicks with me eventually has to stick with me if I want to experience and enjoy lasting change. For me, it is the application that can often be the most challenging. There are many, many "clicks" I encounter throughout a given week or month, but if I am honest, the things that really materialize into lasting changes comprise a far shorter list. What writing in a sense has both offered and exposed is the opportunity to formally put down on paper the things I sense God seeking to change and grow in my own heart and life. I am faced with the same challenge as every reader—what is God revealing in me that I need His help to reshape?

Blame it on nearing the mid-century age or maybe just the current, unstable state of the world, but I am finding myself with an increased sense of urgency to not waste any more time. I need things God has in mind for me and my life to click and stick. God is not a god of chaos or uncertainty—everything His hands have ever touched have been ordered and purposeful. My human tendencies continue to be my biggest obstacle to this custom-built life of God-honoring greatness. It is "go-time" for me and for you—let's be on point and be on the Kingdom mission as we live out the lives He intended and as we draw others to Him.

Printed in the USA
CPSIA information can be obtained
at www.ICGtesting.com
LVHW050919201124
797126LV00004B/183